Unmasked!

Unmasked!

Recognizing and Dealing with Imposters in the Church

by

O. S. Hawkins

MOODY PRESS
CHICAGO

All Scripture quotations are from *The Holy Bible, New King James Version* © 1979, 1980, 1982, by Thomas Nelson, Inc. Used by permission.

Library of Congress Cataloging in Publication Data

Hawkins, O. S.
    Unmasked! / by O.S. Hawkins.
      p.   cm.
    ISBN 0-8024-1692-6
    1. Christianity—20th century. 2. Apostasy. 3. Christian
life—1960-   I. Title.
BR121.2.H3553   1989
270.8'2—dc20   89-3290
                                           CIP

2 3 4 5 6 7 8 Printing/BC/Year 94 93 92 91 90 89

Printed in the United States of America

DEDICATION

To Wendy:

Our "first born." Her commitment, her courage, and her convictions are everything for which a Dad could hope and pray. In fact, if I had to put in words what I wanted in a daughter, I would simply write what she is! Wendy, I am very proud to be your Dad!

CONTENTS

FOREWORD

Only once in a great while does a book appear that speaks so pointedly and prophetically at such a controversial issue as does *UNMASKED! . . . Recognizing and Dealing with Imposters in the Church.* It is a book for our time and sounds the alarm of apostasy which has so subtly invaded our churches, schools, and denominations. It is a "call to arms" for the church as we move toward the twenty-first century.

Dr. O. S. Hawkins's church is the embodiment of what he preaches and writes. This gifted Bible expositor is being used of God to build one of America's great churches in one of the country's most unique and challenging cities, Fort Lauderdale, Florida. It has been my delight on occasion to preach from his pulpit as he has from mine. His church wins to Christ and disciples between five-hundred and one thousand new adult converts annually. Perhaps one of the surest signs of God's blessing upon this fellowship is in the scores of its members who have sensed God's call to vocational ministry and have gone to the ends of the earth sharing the good news of the Lord Jesus Christ.

The principles that follow in this volume are not second-hand, but rather have been beaten out on the anvil of personal experience. I happily and heartily commend this book to every believer. It is a book for our time. It is a call to action. We alone will be responsible "if the foundations be destroyed."

Charles F. Stanley
Atlanta, Georgia

PREFACE

Three thousand years ago King David asked a probing question, "If the foundations be destroyed, what shall the righteous do?" (Psalm 11:3). In this day and age many of our ethical and ecclesiastical foundations are crumbling before our eyes. Some denominations, schools, and churches that were once alive and vibrant are now dead or dying. Satan sought to destroy the early church from without, but the blood of the martyrs became the seed of church growth. In these last days, his strategy is to destroy the church within through apostasy (a falling away from the truth). This volume is designed for anyone, anywhere who takes seriously the admonition to "contend earnestly for the faith which was once for all delivered to the saints" (Jude 3).

As I began the penning of this volume, I became aware of the possibility of appearing to be an alarmist. But as each passing month brings more reports of dying denominations, pastor's scandals, moral failures, and so many churches making such little impact in society, these words are sadly not so much alarmism as realism. What should be our response as concerned churchmen? Should we stand by idly, going along with the crowd or should we seek to stand against the tide and "speak the truth in love"? If I had to reduce this preface to one challenge, it would be a challenge to "contend earnestly for the faith which was once for all delivered to the saints." As we journey together across these pages, every word is designed, not only to sound the alarm, but to equip each of us to defend the faith in days of apostasy.

I am indebted to many people who, in their own unique and diversified ways, have made this volume a reality. First, the three ladies in my life (Susie, my wife; and Wendy and Holly, my daughters) who have allowed me time in the evenings to study and write. As the Lord has enlarged our personal ministry, they have never complained about sharing me with others. This volume would not have been a reality without my secretary, Wanda Todd's loyalty and dedication. I am especially grateful for the encouragement of my friend and spiritual confidant, Dr. George Sweeting, Chancellor of Moody Bible Institute, a "Barnabas" in the truest sense. Also, my appreciation goes to my friends at Moody Press and in particular Dana Gould, whose editorial suggestions have proven invaluable.

Let's begin the journey with the prayer that those who do seek, knowingly or unknowingly, to "destroy the foundations" of our faith might be once and for all . . . unmasked!

O. S. Hawkins
First Baptist Church
Fort Lauderdale, Florida

ONE
THE SIEGE WITHIN

Eli Cohen. Those knowledgeable of the last forty years of Israeli history know his name well. He was born in 1924 in the Jewish quarter of Alexandria, Egypt, the son of a Jewish silk tiemaker. Cohen worked hard to obtain an education. He excelled as a student, becoming fluent in many languages.

War came to Egypt in the 1940s. Soon Cohen found himself drawn to political causes and he became involved with the Egyptian branch of the Mossad Aliyah Beth, an organization that smuggled immigrating Jews past British officials. In the ensuing years Cohen supported many Israeli causes and developed an expertise in espionage. To the Mossad (the Israeli Intelligence Agency), Cohen was a valuable man, for during the course of his covert activities and support of Israel he maintained his outstanding credentials as an Egyptian.

In 1961 the Mossad sent Cohen to Damascus, Syria, to pose as a wealthy Arab businessman with holdings in Buenos Aires, Argentina. He quickly engaged himself in the import-export business. After securing an apartment in the wealthiest sector of Damascus, he soon began giving large sums of money to Syrian politicians, who in turn gave him entree into high political and social circles. He was a regular guest at presidential palace parties and became a personal confidant of many government leaders. It was not unusual for him to be taken on high-level briefings at the Syrian-Israeli border.

In those days Israel was dependent on pipelines in Galilee for its water supply. The pipelines passed through the Golan Heights region, which was under Syrian control. Cohen discovered that the Syrians were preparing to implement a plan to cut off the water supply to Israel.

During a visit to the Syrian frontier, Cohen convinced President Al-Hafez to plant eucalyptus trees at major military installations on the Golan Heights. The trees would provide good cover and shield the installations from Israeli air surveillance while Syria proceeded to carry out its plan.

Eli Cohen's life of espionage was uncovered in 1965, and he was hanged as a spy in the town square of Damascus. A few months later, during the famous Six-Day War, Israeli fighter pilots had little trouble knocking out all the Syrian targets on the Golan Heights because of previous information supplied by Cohen. They simply looked for patches of eucalyptus trees!

The Golan Heights are in control of the State of Israel today because of an imposter who provided valuable intelligence information to Israel while posing as a wealthy Arab businessman in Syria.

An imposter who has infiltrated an organization can play out his agenda long before he is detected. That is the warning to the church we find in the epistle of Jude. In Jude's words, "Certain men have crept in unnoticed, who long ago were marked out for this condemnation, ungodly men, who turn the grace of our God into lewdness and deny the only Lord God and our Lord Jesus Christ" (v. 4). Left to his work, an imposter can threaten the mission and very life of any organization.

Although, because of its vulnerability, the church is constantly under the threat of siege by infiltration, it is not defenseless. It can preserve the faith from corruption and destruction by recognizing and properly dealing with imposters. Those of us who are true believers can begin by gaining helpful perspectives on the problem of apostasy in the church.

WHAT IS AN IMPOSTER?

An imposter is someone who claims to be someone or something he is not. In the context of the body of Christ, he is one who claims to be a believer. He is one who has received in some way the truth of the written Word, but not the living Word, the Lord Jesus Christ. His "Christianity" is theoretical, not experiential. He is what the epistle of Jude calls an *apostate.*

Apostates claim to be Christians, but they are not. But neither are they merely unbelievers. Apostates are those who know the truth but do not act upon it. They perform an inside job and are tools of the enemy to destroy the foundation of the church even though they themselves may be blind to this reality.

Judas, the apostle, is an excellent example of an imposter. Although he claimed to be a believer, he was not. He had achieved near-perfect attendance with our Lord and His band of disciples for three-and-a-half years. In fact, he had appeared so trustworthy that he was appointed treasurer of that entourage! Judas's foundational problem was that he had seen the light, but did not have the life.

THE CHURCH'S ONGOING BATTLE

Imposters are at work today. Their strategy is destruction by infiltration. Like Eli Cohen, they have crept in unnoticed and seek to destroy the work of God from within. Our denominations, organizations, Christian colleges and seminaries are their victims.

In the early days of the church, believers met tremendous opposition from the outside. Satan tried to destroy the church from without by means of persecution. History shows that persecution has not worked to destroy the church; rather, the blood of the martyrs has been the seed of church growth. The more the church has been persecuted, the more it has flourished.

In our generation we have seen this phenomenon occur in mainland China. Although the church in China has seen persecution for decades, it is not defeated—it is stronger! It seems that in these last days Satan's strategy is taking on a renewed emphasis. He seeks to not only destroy the church from without, but to also do so *from within*. His target is the Word of God, the foundation of our faith, upon which the church is built. It is no wonder that Jude admonishes us: "Beloved, while I was very diligent to write to you concerning our common salvation, I found it necessary to write to you exhorting you to contend earnestly for the faith which was once for all delivered to the saints" (Jude 3).

The work of infiltrators takes the life and heart from the church. There are many denominations and organizations that can attest to that today. Once they were thriving, vibrant, and alive, but now they are dead or dying. What happened? It certainly didn't happen from caving in to outside pressures. It happened from within! Imposters— those who have turned from the truth—have "crept in unnoticed" and are about the business of destroying the foundation from within.

Lessons from History

One of the most used platforms of imposter activity is the field of education. Institutions of higher learning such as Harvard, Yale, Brown, Dartmouth, Princeton have much in common. Yes, they are all Ivy League schools. They have ongoing traditions. But their one forgotten common element is that they were all founded for the express purpose of the propagation of the gospel of the Lord Jesus Christ. They were established for the glory of God. Tragically, they each left their calling.

WARNING FROM THE BIBLE

The Bible is relevant to the current issue of imposter infiltration. That is why it is important for the church today to consider the warnings of Jude. The book of Jude was originally written to Jewish Christians to counter the heresy of Gnosticism, a false teaching that had crept into the early church. Today we are just as vulnerable (if not more so) to falling prey to false teaching and subversive doctrines. The warning of apostasy is applicable to Christians everywhere and at any time during this present Church Age.

The book of Jude is clear in its warnings about apostasy. An apostate turned imposter is dangerous to the church and needs to be reckoned with. The warning that should shake the church into action is that it can expect apostates, in the form of imposters, to infiltrate its ranks and leadership positions.

In his first letter to Timothy Paul joins Jude in reminding us that "in latter times some will depart from the faith" (1 Timothy 4:1). The message of Jude joins hands with other epistles in the New Testament to sound the alarm and wake the church out of its slumber that it might "earnestly contend for the faith which was once for all delivered to the saints."

CONCLUSION

Eli Cohen, as an imposter, sneaked into a foreign country and set out to destroy its foundations. As damaging as he was to the Syrian cause, he was not nearly as destructive as those of Satan's secret service today who have infiltrated unnoticed into our churches, schools, and organizations seeking to destroy their foundations by casting doubt upon the authority and infallibility of the Word of God. If an imposter was able to infiltrate Jesus' band of disciples, should we be surprised that the church of Jesus Christ today stands vulnerable to Satan's work of infiltration?

More than three thousand years ago, King David asked a very probing question, "If the foundations are destroyed, what can the righteous do?" (Psalm 11:3). Today many of our ethical and ecclesiastical foundations are crumbling before our eyes. Some denominations, schools, and churches that once held the Bible in high regard seem now to have little respect for it. Jude gives a clear call to the believer to earnestly contend for the faith, the Word of God. If our generation fails to contend for this faith which has been delivered unto us, we, the church of Jesus Christ, will be held accountable.

TWO
BEWARE OF IMPOSTERS!

Have you ever held a counterfeit bill? It can have all the appearances and feel of the real thing. Most people are not able to immediately recognize one. However, a trained eye can quickly detect fake currency, because certain telltale flaws betray a bill's lack of genuineness.

United States law enforcement takes effective measures to prevent counterfeit currency activity. Strict and severe penalties are imposed on those who disregard laws against generating counterfeit money. The reason is obvious. Left unchecked, widespread counterfeit currency would be devastating to our economy.

In a similar way, counterfeit Christians are devastating to the church. To protect its integrity the church must take the responsibility of discerning between true and false believers.

Before we can recognize an imposter, we must first be able to contrast him to his authentic counterpart. That is, we need to know how a counterfeit Christian differs from a genuine believer. Such an understanding will better enable us to discern between the two.

The Genuine Believer

The genuine believer is different than his counterfeit counterpart for at least two reasons—who he is and what he has.

WHO HE IS

Three facts from Scripture help us understand who the genuine believer is. According to the book of Jude we know that he is uniquely embraced by the Godhead—the Father, Son, and Holy Spirit. First, authentic believers are *called* by the Holy Spirit (Jude 1). The word *called* means "an official summons." Genuine believers have been summoned by God. Salvation begins with God. (If it began with us, we could lose it!) The apostle Peter reminds us that we are "a chosen generation, a royal priesthood, a holy nation, His own special people, that you may proclaim the praises of Him who has called us out of darkness into His marvelous light" (1 Peter 2:9).

I remember the day God called me. I had heard the outward call of the gospel many times before, but that day I heard the inward call. A seventeen-year-old young man came out of spiritual death into spiritual life. Like Lydia in the book of Acts "whose heart the Lord opened," God called me out of darkness into His marvelous light. We know from Scripture that every true believer has been called from death unto life.

Second, true believers are *beloved* by God the Father. Those who are beloved are set apart for God Himself. He called us and brought us out of the world, washed us in His blood, and now sets us apart for Himself. Love has a way of setting one's beloved apart. When a man loves a woman and marries her, he sets her apart from all others for his very own. Although God loves all people, only genuine believers are His beloved.

Jesus alluded to this point in His high priestly intercessory prayer on the evening before His crucifixion. He prayed for us as He petitioned the Father:

> I do not pray for these alone, but also for those who will believe in Me through their word; that they all may be one, as You, Father are in Me, and I in You; that they also may be one in Us that the world may believe that you sent Me. And the glory which You gave Me, I have given them, that they may be one just as We are one; I in them, and You in Me; that they may be made perfect in one, and that the world may know that You have sent Me, and have loved them as You have loved Me. [John 17:20-23]

An earthly parent's love is sometimes conditional. Not so with God. As His children we can do nothing to make God love us more or less than He loves us already. He does not love us because we are valuable or worthy. We are valuable and worthy *because He loves us.* The Bible tells us that nothing can separate us from this love.

Our Father's love is beyond comparison. His children are precious to Him. The apostle John comments on this truth when he says, "Behold what manner of love the Father has bestowed on us, that we should be called children of God" (1 John 3:1). We parents often think about how much we love our children, and the truth is that our heavenly Father loves us even more.

Third, the genuine believer is "preserved in Jesus Christ" (Jude 1) and kept by the Father. The word *preserved* is the Greek word *tereō* , which means "to watch, to guard over."[1] In its original language text, the word appears in the perfect tense, which indicates past completed action with continuing results. It might best be translated "continually kept." So when a believer stumbles He has the assurance that God keeps him from falling.

I remember when our little daughter began to walk.

She would reach up with her chubby little fingers, grab my index finger, and hang on with all her might. After only a step or two, she would let go and fall to the ground. It wasn't long before I learned an important lesson. If *I* reached down and took hold of her hand, I would be there to hold her up and teach her to walk. And if she stumbled, I could keep her from falling. What a perfect analogy of how our heavenly Father helps us. Our salvation is not a matter of our holding on till the bitter end. No. He reaches down and grabs hold of us, and when we stumble, He is there to help us along. I would do anything to keep one of my children from falling, and I am only human. How much more does God the Father want to keep us from falling.

The apostle Paul said, "For this reason I also suffer these things; nevertheless I am not ashamed, for I know whom I have believed and am persuaded that He is able to keep what I have committed to Him until that Day" (2 Timothy 1:12). Whereas apostates sin, fall, and suffer condemnation, true believers are kept forever.

The writer of Hebrews tells how we are kept: "He is also able to save to the uttermost those who come to God through Him, since He always lives to make intercession for them" (Hebrews 7:25).[2] We believers need to take comfort in the fact that Jesus prays for us. He started His prayer, for us the evening before His crucifixion when He prayed, "Now I am no longer in the world, but these are in the world and I come to You. Holy Father, keep through Your name those whom You have given Me that they may be one as We are" (John 17:11). Jude sums up his epistle by saying, "Now to Him who is able to keep you from stumbling, and to present you faultless before the presence of His glory with exceeding joy" (v. 24). Those verses also emphasize *who* keeps us. It is God the Father who keeps us; not we ourselves.

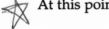 At this point we should remind ourselves that an apos-

tate is not simply a true believer who walks away from his
salvation. That is impossible according to Scripture. To the
contrary, an apostate is one who professes Christ as Savior
but does not possess Christ as Savior. The apostle Peter
made it clear that apostates where not like God's sheep, but
instead like pigs and dogs when he said:

> For it would have been better for them not to have known the
> way of righteousness, than having known it, to turn from the
> holy commandment delivered to them. But it has happened
> to them according to the true proverb: "A dog returns to his
> own vomit," and, "a sow, having washed, to her wallowing in
> the mire." [2 Peter 2:21-22]

We might be able to clean up a pig on the outside, take
it to the county fair and show it off, but that will not change
its nature. The pig will go right back to the mire and slop of
the pigpen as soon as it has opportunity.

So we know a true believer by who he is. He is the
recipient of God's care and protection. That is, he is called
by the Holy Spirit, beloved by the Father, and kept by the
Son.

WHAT HE HAS

As true believers we are recipients of three important
gifts—mercy, peace, and love. All true believers receive
them because they are by-products of our sanctification.
These gifts are very important as we seek to evangelize the
world.

Jude made an interesting request regarding those gifts.
He asked God to multiply them toward us. Perhaps the only
way the church is to cope with the apostasy of these last
days is to have mercy, peace, and love multiplied to us.
These gifts, in effect, become the weapons that help us win

against imposters. I believe that the shortest way to see the salvation of sinners is to let them see the sanctification of true believers at work.

The genuine believer exhibits the gifts of mercy, peace, and love continually as these gifts are borne out in the three basic relationships in life.

Our relationship with God. This is the upward expression. As a result of this relationship true believers receive mercy from above. This is why the writer of Hebrews exhorts us to "come boldly to the throne of grace, that we might obtain mercy and find grace to help in time of need" (Hebrews 4:16). God, in His mercy, does not give us what we deserve. Instead, morning by morning new mercies we see! God is rich in mercy and chooses not to withold it from us. This is important, because it is God's mercy that continues to forgive our sin.

Our relationship with ourselves. This is the inward expression. Because we receive mercy from God we can have peace within ourselves. The upward expression must precede the inward expression. Many people are searching, groping, and struggling for inner peace and never find it, because it only comes after one receives mercy from God. Jesus said, "Peace I leave with you, My peace I give to you; not as the world gives do I give to you. Let not your heart be troubled, neither let it be afraid" (John 14:27). The only way we can have peace within is first to be at peace with God. If you do not have this peace it is because you have not received God's mercy.

Our relationship with others. If we have received mercy from God and are at peace with ourselves, we can love others as Jesus commanded. The evening before His crucifixion Jesus gave us a new commandment, "A new commandment I give to you, that you love one another; as I have loved you, that you also love one another. By this all will know that you are My disciples if you have love for one another" (John 13:34-35). This love is known as agape love. It is the bond that unites believers to the Lord and to one another.

Imposters are void of such love. They may be professors of Christianity, but they are not possessors of Christ. They simply cannot love on the agape level. The outward expression (love) depends on the inward expression (peace), which depends on the upward expression (mercy). The only way to love others is to be at peace with self, and the only way we can be at peace with self is to accept mercy from the Father. False believers have yet to experience God's mercy.

THE BASIC DIFFERENCES

Imposters are exact opposites of the true believer.
- The believer is called by the Holy Spirit; the imposter is not
- The believer is kept by God; the imposter is lost
- The believer receives mercy from God; the imposter receives no mercy
- The believer has peace within; the imposter lives a lie
- The believer expresses love toward others; the imposter is self-seeking and deceitful
- The believer has mercy, peace, and love multiplied to him; the imposter has no such gifts multiplied to him

Imposters are not genuine believers. They have never known the mercy of God, and consequently live a lie without any real peace within. Because they do not know the Lord Jesus Christ personally, they cannot love on His level. In short, they are false prophets.

To "earnestly contend for the faith" it is imperative that a believer knows what he has in Christ. It is he who can show the love of Christ to those who need God's mercy.

DETECTING COUNTERFEIT CHRISTIANS

A recent edition of the *Fort Lauderdale News* carried the story of a local bank robbery. Accompanying the article was a picture taken by the bank's security camera. It showed the robber dressed in full disguise, which included a hat, glasses, and what was obviously, a false mustache. He had changed his appearance cosmetically so as to hide his real identity.

The word *cosmetic* comes from the Greek word *kosmetikos*, which means "a decorating or covering over." It is to dress up something to give it an appearance on the surface that is unlike its reality.

The Bible tells us that spiritual criminals, cosmetically disguised, are seeking to rob the church of power and blessing. The book of Jude speaks of imposters who disguise themselves to look authentic; who infiltrate the church and bring confusion and conflict. These imposters (or apostates) are merely pretenders. They know the truth and even embrace it. They are "into" religion. But they know nothing about a relationship with Jesus Christ.

Every believer needs to be on alert. Spiritual criminals are among us—in our churches, our schools, denominations, and organizations.

IMPOSTERS ARE EASILY DETECTED

The Bible reveals to us that those whose faith and fellowship are merely cosmetic are easily detected. Jude uses five metaphors to reveal the true character of these infiltrators. He refers to them as hidden rocks, clouds without water, trees without fruit, raging waves of the sea, and wandering stars.

Imposters lack peace. A cosmetic Christian is like a hidden rock in a love feast (see Jude 12). The picture here is one of a large rock or reef just below the surface of the water where it cannot be seen by the naked eye.

Those of you who live near large bodies of water may have had the experience of being on a boat run aground. Perhaps you were skimming along on top of the water when the boat lurched, came to a sudden halt, and water began to seep in from the bottom of the hull. A quick inspection revealed that a rock hidden beneath the surface of the water did the damage.

As a sea captain pilots his vessel he is not concerned with the reefs and rocks clearly marked on his navigation charts. It is the hidden rocks and reefs that concern him, for they are unseen.

The Bible warns us that cosmetic Christians are like hidden rocks "in our love feasts." Tertullian, in his defense of Christianity before the Roman government in A.D. 197, describes the love feasts Jude mentions. In the early days of the church was a weekly gathering called the love feast. It amounted to a large fellowship meal in which everyone shared food, fun, and fellowship together. The rich and the poor, the young and the old alike gathered for this happy occasion.

However, love feasts eventually ceased because imposters infiltrated the church and turned the love feasts into cliques. The feasts served to simply further the imposters' selfish ambitions. In some cases those church gatherings degenerated into drunken orgies. In his first letter to the Corinthians, Paul rebuked them severely for allowing the feast to be characterized by shameful drunkenness and immorality.

A major problem with imposters in the church is that they are unseen dangers. They often do their damage before they are detected. False doctrines and selfish motives lie just below the surface. Like rocks and reefs under the water they tear up the fellowship and destroy love within the church.

Satan plants his "hidden rocks" to cause division and

dissension. They are unseen at first, but before long the fellowship runs aground. Wise pastors and leaders learn to steer their churches and organizations around such hidden dangers.

Discord, division, and dissension stymie church growth. I am convinced that love and unity among the fellowship of believers is the most important factor in church growth. People are seldom saved in churches that do not manifest a sweet fellowship. After all, who wants to be part of a fellowship that is always fussing and fighting?

Cosmetic Christians promote disunity. They are not peace-makers; they are peace-breakers. Our Lord said, "Blessed are the peacemakers, for they shall be called sons of God" (Matthew 5:9). The tragedy of the early church was that believers in many cases did not recognize imposters until they had destroyed the fellowship. How many churches today, sailing across the ocean of love and fellowship, have run aground on cosmetic Christians who, like hidden rocks and sunken reefs, brought discord and dissension. Let us not make the same mistake the early church did.

Imposters lack productivity. They are like "clouds without water, carried about by the winds" (Jude 12). By using the metaphor of empty clouds Jude wants us to know that cosmetic Christians are easily detected by a lack of productivity. Clouds without water are filled only with false promises.

I served my first pastorate in Hobart, Oklahoma, one of the wheat farming centers of the world. The wheat harvest occurs around the first of June. For most of the faithful farmers in that area, their livelihood depends on the June harvest. The harvest is, of course, dependent on ample spring rains.

I remember well one particular year of drought. No rain had fallen for weeks and crops were in desperate need of water. The tanks and reservoirs had run dry. Everything that should have been green was brown. The outlook was bleak.

One day around noon, clouds began to roll in from the south. The whole town went into a frenzy! People gathered on the courthouse lawn to welcome the coming rain. But a strange thing happened. Those long-awaited clouds, with their promise of rain, just sailed on by without depositing a drop. They were filled with promises but did not deliver. And they left a bunch of faithful farmers with nothing but deep disappointment.

To a farmer few things can be as despairing as clouds without water in times of drought. To the church few things can be as despairing as a cosmetic Christian. He has all the looks and sounds, but no substance. He may talk a good game, but his productivity is nil.

Preachers can stand in pulpits and church members sit in pews every Sunday and produce nothing. Imposters are often people with personality and much potential. They are quick to boast of their abilities, but they never produce spiritual fruit. King Solomon said, "Whoever falsely boasts of giving is like clouds and wind without rain" (Proverbs 25:14). Many churches today are pastored by men of great ability who produce nothing but empty promises as they "mouth great swelling words, flattering people to gain advantage" (Jude 16).

These people promote all the latest denominational programs with their catchy slogans. They are filled with promises and new ideas for bigger and better days ahead. But mostly it is just talk. The result is little productivity. These men survive by knowing the right people in the right places. Spiritually starving people sit in some churches week after week listening to clouds without water while thirsting for the water of life. Instead, they hear words without wonders and promises without productivity. The refreshing rain never falls.

Imposters lack proof. Another way imposters can be

easily detected is the fact of no fruit in their lives. They are like "late autumn trees without fruit, twice dead, pulled up by the roots" (Jude 12). In the Middle East the harvest falls well before late Autumn. Late Autumn is the season trees shed their leaves. Therefore, it is not a season when fruit is expected. The picture Jude describes is one of late Autumn trees whose branches are bare and leafless as Winter approaches.[3]

The metaphor Jude uses is accurate, for cosmetic Christians are void of any life-giving sap. They are sterile. As a result they produce no fruit at all. The only way a branch can bring forth fruit is by receiving life from the vine. Cosmetic Christians have no life ("not having the Spirit" [Jude 19]), because they are not attached to the vine by the new birth.

Jude reveals that not only are imposters like trees without fruit, but they are "twice dead." He says "they are pulled up by the roots." In commenting on this passage, Maxwell Coder has said, "They have no fruit of profession because they have no root of possession."[4] All trees look dead in late Autumn, but those with life will bloom again. They only appear dead. However, those twice dead look dead because they are dead. A twice dead tree is both sterile and lifeless.

Such trees are "uprooted." That is, they are torn up by the roots and disposed by burning. John the Baptist referred to this eventuality when he said, "And even now the ax is laid to the root of the trees. Therefore every tree which does not bear good fruit is cut down and thrown into the fire" (Matthew 3:10).

The basic problem with cosmetic Christians is that they are spiritually dead. What can we do with dead trees? We can prune them, but that will not give them life. We can transplant them, but if they are dead, they will not live again. We can cultivate them all we want, but if they are dead, *they are dead*. Jesus said, "If anyone does not abide in me, he is cast out as a branch and is withered; and they gather them and throw them into the fire, and they are burned" (John 15:6).

Cosmetic Christians turned imposter cannot build great schools or growing churches because they have no power in and of themselves. Instead, they attach themselves to schools, churches, and organizations that are built in the life-giving, infallible truth of the Word of God, and begin to suck the life out of them.

Liberal theology cannot produce fruit. It does not build great schools, found growing churches, and energize organizations. But, like a leech, it sucks the life out of many.

Our Lord told the parable of the sower to teach us that the seed that falls on the hard ground, the shallow ground, or the thorny ground brings forth no fruit. The only seed that brings forth fruit is that which is planted in the good ground.

The proof of the Christian life is in the fruit. Jesus said in the Sermon on the Mount, "You will know them by their fruits" (Matthew 7:16). It is one of the obvious evidences of authentic salvation.

Imposters lack purity. They are like "raging waves of the sea, foaming up their own shame" (Jude 13). In other words, they expose themselves. Like wild waves they leave the filth and shame of their innermost being on the shores of life for all to see. They are easily detected by a lack of purity.

In Florida, when the weather is calm, the ocean is crystal clear. But when storms come and the winds of hurricane season blow, the ocean begins to rage and churn. The raging waves bring the filth and debris from the ocean floor and deposits it on the shore. After the storm, the shore fills with beachcombers who find everything from rotting fish to shiny shells.

The cosmetic Christian is like that. He loses his temper when the storm comes, and in a rage reveals the filth that lies on the ocean floor of the innermost recesses of his heart. Long before Jude, Isaiah said it this way, "But the wicked are like the troubled sea, when it cannot rest, whose waters cast up mire and dirt" (Isaiah 57:20). In the heart of the imposter is great turmoil because of the mire and filth in his life. It is only a matter of time before he shows his vile and wicked sin that lies on the ocean floor of his character.

An interesting correlation exists with cosmetic Christians. Throughout the Bible, apostasy and sensual sin go hand in hand. Imposters seem to exercise little moral restraint. We need to keep in mind that an apostate is not simply an unbeliever. He is one who knows the truth and turns away from it, and in doing so, opens his life to all sorts of immoral sins, which Jude says are to his "own shame." This a repetitive truth throughout Jude's epistle. He says that apostates

> Turn the grace of our God into lewdness. . . . As Sodom and Gomorrah and the cities around them in a similar manner to these, having given themselves over to sexual immorality and gone after strange flesh, are set forth as an example. Likewise, also these dreamers defile the flesh. [Jude 4, 7-8]

I have watched many men preach who knew the truth in their minds but did not have it in their hearts. They soon began to deny the inerrancy of Scripture or the virgin birth. They didn't want to leave "religion," but they went down one by one in divorce, immorality, and homosexuality. Eventually imposters expose themselves, and the filth of their life washes up on the shore for all to see.

Imposters lack purpose. They are like "wandering stars for whom is reserved the blackness of darkness forever" (Jude 13). They have no real direction in life; no purpose. For a while they flicker, and then God has a way darkening their existence.

One of my fondest childhood memories is of lying on my back on a pallet during hot Summer nights in the backyard of our home. (That was before the days of air conditioning, color television, and videos.) I will never forget looking up at the stars and learning about the Milky Way and the Big Dipper and the Little Dipper. As a family we spent hours just gazing into the heavens. Then one night it happened. Racing across the sky was a shooting star. Its brillance was dazzling. As quickly as it appeared, it disappeared into the darkness of the night.

God placed all the stars in their courses in the heavens. We know that not only from astronomy, but also from Scripture that reveals "they fought from the heavens; the stars from their courses fought against Sisera" (Judges 5:20). Stars are set in their course. They have orbits. They have direction and purpose.

Cosmetic Christians are like wandering stars, with no purpose or direction. They make a big flash and then disappear. Like burned out chunks of rock, they are hurled into the dark recesses of space. They are stars out of orbit.

A good sea captain will know the heavens like the back of his hand. His experience tells him to ignore wandering stars when he sees them. He makes his nocturnal navigational decisions by the stars that have order, the ones that are always in their proper place.

The fact is that cosmetic Christians do not want to be in an orbit. They do not like structures or statements of faith. They do not want to be fenced in or play within any set boundaries. They lack purpose.

Sadly, it is a bitter end for the apostate. His destination is the "blackness of darkness forever." To me, the most haunting aspect of hell is its darkness. Can you imagine how it must be to be conscious and in complete, total darkness forever? Let a power failure cause a few moments of darkness and people panic. But imagine the impact of darkness forever.

We have seen men and women with much promise and

potential who blazed brilliantly for a moment and then fell into the darkness. God has His way of dealing with cosmetic Christians. He is still in control.

The church needs be on the watch for those who would destroy the fellowship of love. Be assured that we can detect imposters because we know what characterizes them.

ENDNOTES:

1. John MacArthur, Jr., *Beware the Pretenders* (Wheaton, Ill.: Victor Books, 1980), p. 17.

2. Charles H. Spurgeon, *The Treasury of the New Testament*, 4 vols. (Grand Rapids: Zondervan, 1950), 4:628.

3. J. N. D. Kelly, *A Commentary on the Epistle of Peter and Jude* (Grand Rapids: Baker, 1969), p. 272.

4. Maxwell Coder, *Jude, the Acts of the Apostates* (Chicago: Moody, 1958), p. 79.

THREE
ANATOMY OF AN APOSTATE

F ort Lauderdale, Florida, is primarily known for its beautiful beaches and miles of waterways within its city limits. What is not commonly known about Fort Lauderdale is that it is also the home of one of the world's largest swapshops.

I've passed by that swap-shop a thousand times. Some time ago I decided to stop in and look around. As I passed by one booth I could not believe my eyes. Beautiful namebrand watches were selling for a fraction of their retail cost. Remembering that my wife's birthday was rapidly approaching, I purchased one of the watches that normally carried a price tag of several hundred dollars, for the mere sum of fifteen dollars. I rushed home and proudly presented it to her as a birthday gift.

Later that evening during dinner, my wife looked at her new watch to check the time and discovered the second hand going berserk. Then it stopped dead in its tracks. Although the watch looked like the real thing in every respect, it was a fake. It did not stand up under pressure.

THE PARABLE OF THE SOWER

Such is true of the apostate. This is the point Jesus was making when He told the parable of the sower in Luke 8.

The apostate is like the seed sown on rocky ground. This person, when he hears, receives the word with joy but has no roots. For a while he believes, but soon temptation wins out and he "falls away." The phrase "fall away" in Luke 8:13 is the verb form of "apostasy."

Luke's choice of words in the original Greek language is interesting. Referring to the stony ground hearers who "receive the word" in Luke 8:13, the word is *dekomai*. He uses a different word to describe the good ground hearers who also receive the word. The word for "receive" found in Mark 4:20, which is used of the good ground hearers, is the word *paradekomai*. It is a much stronger word than *dekomai* and indicates that these people truly welcome the word into their hearts, whereas the stony ground hearers do so superficially.

Stony ground hearers fall away from the truth because they have no roots. Consequently, they have no fruit. Absence of fruit is absence of evidence of the Christian life. An apostate knows the truth but does not apply it. He "accepts" God's revelation as true but does not make a sincere commitment to it.

A truly born-again person cannot become an apostate. Although he may fall into error or into indifference, he cannot fall away from the faith. Scripture is clear in assuring us that Jesus is able to keep us forever.

In the previous chapter we learned something of the outward characteristics of a cosmetic Christian. A knowledge of those will certainly help us detect imposters. In this chapter we will examine the activities that betray the apostate. We will discover what makes this kind of person "tick."

THE APOSTATE'S "AGENDA"

We can best defend against apostates by understanding the nature of their activities.

THE APOSTATE'S DECEITFULNESS

Apostates creep in. Jude 4 says that "certain men have crept in unnoticed." The word *crept* means to "slip in secretly, to steal in under cover."[1] The word describing this action carries the idea of slipping in the back door. It is used to speak of one who slips back secretly into a country from which he was expelled. It also paints the picture of an alligator, lying on the bank of a river, and then slithering into the river so subtly, secretly, and silently that he is unnoticed.

These synthetic saints creep into denominations, churches, schools, and organizations. They are in our Sunday school classes, choirs, pews, classrooms, and pulpits. And they are deceitful. Jesus warned us about them and how they deceive when He said, "Beware of false prophets, who come to you in sheep's clothing, but inwardly they are ravenous wolves" (Matthew 7:15).

The result of an apostate's deceitfulness is destruction. Consider the field of higher education. Of the first one hundred colleges founded in America, eighty-eight were founded for the propagation of the gospel of the Lord Jesus Christ. Today, few, if any, of those schools still carry that mission.

Recently, Harvard University celebrated its 350th birthday. When Harvard was founded in 1636, all its students held to three basic rules. First, everyone was to consider it the main end of his studies to know God and eternal life through the Lord Jesus Christ. Second, because according to Scripture the Lord gives wisdom, every student was to seek the wisdom of God. Third, every student was to exercise himself in the reading of the Scriptures twice a day so that he could give an account of his profession. That was the aim of the school in its beginning days. That aim has since been abandoned.

What has happened to our schools that were founded

on the fundamentals of the faith? Some denominations that founded them have gone the way of apostasy. Jude says that happens because imposters creep in unnoticed and destroy them. That is why we need to contend for the faith today. What were once great, strong schools producing missionaries who went around the world are now dead or dying. And the destruction continues.

Who would have dreamed even a few years ago that Darwinian evolution would be taught in the classrooms of some of our institutions of higher learning? Who would have believed that "conservative" theologians would deny the miracles of the Old Testament? It will not be long before they will deny the miracles of the New Testament, which include the resurrection of our Lord Jesus Christ.

Dr. L. R. Scarborough was the second president of what is now the largest theological seminary in the world, Southwestern Baptist Seminary in Fort Worth, Texas. Scarborough relates one of his conversations with the founding president, Dr. B. H. Carroll. In his book, *Gospel Message*, Scarborough tells of going to Dr. Carroll's room a few days before Carroll's death. As they conversed Carroll pulled himself up from the pillow and looked into Scarborough's face and said, "My boy, on this seminary hill, orthodoxy, the old truth, is making one of its last stands. I want to deliver you a charge and I do it in the blood of Jesus Christ. I want you, if there ever comes heresy in your faculty, to take it to your faculty. If they don't hear you, take it the trustees. If they don't hear you, take it to the conventions that appointed them. If they don't hear you, take it to the common Baptists. They will hear you."

And he concluded, "I charge you in the name of the Lord Jesus Christ to keep it lashed to the old Gospel of Jesus Christ. As long as I have influence in that institution, by the grace of God, I will stand by the old book."[2] These are our roots. Men like Carroll were men who earnestly contended "for the faith which was once for all delivered to the saints."

THE APOSTATE'S DEVOTION

Jude called apostates "ungodly men." Thayer's *Lexicon* defines the underlying Greek word as "destitute of reverential awe toward God." It is lack of what we call "the fear of God." Such men have a form of godliness but deny its power (see 2 Timothy 3:5). A godly man walks with God and knows God. An ungodly man is the opposite.

Jude was not speaking about outward appearances. Apostates are not openly and blatantly ungodly. They look and act like Christians. They may even appear to be good in the eyes of men. Rather, Jude was talking about the heart— the part that only God can see.

All apostates talk about God. They know the language. They may be gifted individuals. They may even be courteous, gentle, and generous. But their hearts are far from God. The apostle Paul warned us about these synthetic saints when he said, "For the time will come when they will not endure sound doctrine, but according to their own desires, because they have itching ears, they will heap up for themselves teachers; and they will turn their ears away from the truth, and be turned aside to fables" (2 Timothy 4:3-4).

Apostasy began in the Garden of Eden when Satan spoke to Eve and questioned the Word of God. Eve knew the word to be true, but Satan planted the seed of doubt when he subtly asked, "Has God said?" But Eve, knowing the truth, moved away from the truth. That spirit of apostasy continues today through the mouths of liberal professors and preachers who question the Word of God with the same words, "Has God said?"

Apostates are not devoted to the cause of Christ. While they may claim to love our Lord, they do not obey Him. They claim to serve Him, but work to serve their own selfish interests. They can severely damage the cause of Christ because they hold leadership positions in our churches, schools, and organizations. The devotion of the apostate is summed up well in the words of Titus 1:16: "They profess to know God, but in works they deny Him, being abominable, disobedient, and disqualified for every good work."

An apostate turns "the grace of God into lewdness" (Jude 4). The word *lewdness* means "an absence of moral restraint." Jude is describing a person who arrogantly flaunts his sin. Such a person does evil deeds without shame. He believes that he can sin all he likes because God will forgive him. That is, the more he sins, the greater God's grace. That kind of thinking turns the grace of God into lewdness because it perverts the doctrine of grace into a justification for sin.

Consider a professing Christian who believes he can do whatever he pleases and indulges in fleshly desires because he is "under" the grace of God. He rationalizes sexual promiscuity by saying, "We are just two vulnerable human beings. God's grace is big enough to cover our sin; He'll forgive us." I am afraid for anyone who thinks that way. Such a person knows nothing of the grace of God.

Paul was clear in his teaching about the grace of God. In writing to Titus he said, "For the grace of God that brings salvation has appeared to all men, teaching us that, denying ungodliness and worldly lusts, we should live soberly, righteously, and godly in the present age, looking for the blessed hope and glorious appearing of our great God and Savior Jesus Christ" (Titus 2:11-13).

God's grace is unmerited favor. It does not lead us to sin. Apostates assume that their privileges in the faith somehow put them above the moral responsibility of the Word of God that binds true believers to life-styles of godliness and purity. The grace of God does quite the contrary. It leads us to deny ungodliness and worldly lusts and to live righteously. When this precious truth is perverted into a license to sin, apostasy has set in.

The writer of Hebrews gives a solemn warning for those who turn the grace of God into lewdness. He says, "O, how much worse punishment, do you suppose, will he be thought worthy who has trampled the Son of God underfoot, counted the blood of the covenant by which he was sanctified a common thing, and insulted the Spirit of grace?" (Hebrews 10:29). It is a dangerous thing to insult the Spirit of grace by using liberty in Christ as license to sin. Certainly, it is one of the most distinguishing characteristics of apostasy.

THE APOSTATE'S DOCTRINE

The apostate denys "the only Lord God and our Lord Jesus Christ" (Jude 4). Here is the root of the problem! He does not deny our Lord with his lips; rather, he denies our Lord with his life.

The Romans had a clever way of appeasing their conquered peoples. They built the Pantheon, a temple to the gods. In it were niches for all the gods and goddesses of the peoples conquered by the Romans. For example, followers of the god Jupiter could come to the Pantheon and worship him. Niche after niche contained gods. When the Romans conquered the Christians they offered to create a niche for Jesus. But the Christians said no, because they believed in only one God.

In fact, Christians insisted that there was only one true God to the point that they would not even bow down to the image of Caesar. Many paid with their lives. We know well the accounts of early Christians who were ripped apart by lions and burned at the stake because they insisted on the fact that there was "only one Lord God and our Lord Jesus Christ."

Today it is heartbreaking to hear of professors in our Christian schools espousing universalist philosophies and doctrines, many discounting a belief in hell altogether. I remember watching a nationally televised talk show in which a Christian educator affirmed that some of his friends who had rejected Jesus Christ would be in heaven and that he would see them there. The Bible says, "There is no other name under heaven given among men by which we must be saved (Acts 4:12)." Of course, that name is Jesus.

THE CHALLENGE BEFORE US

God hates apostasy. The greatest sin of all is to deny the Lord Jesus Christ. Apostates deny Him as Master. They deny Him as Mediator. They deny Him as Messiah. Notice that digression. The first step to becoming ungodly is to have no fear of God; no reverential awe. Second, the precious doctrine of grace is perverted into an excuse to sin. That leads to an outright denial of our only Lord and Savior, Jesus Christ.

What work the devil cannot do from without, he seeks to do from within through synthetic saints. They are deceitful. They creep in unnoticed. Their devotion is ungodly. Their demeanor gives them away. They turn the grace of God into lewdness and their doctrine is the denial of our only Lord Jesus Christ. We must not relax our efforts to recognize these imposters among us.

ENDNOTES:

1. Warren Wiersbe, *Be Alert* (Wheaton, Ill.: Victor Books, 1984), p. 133.

2. Lee Scarborough, *Gospel Messages*. (Nashville: Broadman, 1922), p. 122.

FOUR
DEFENDING THE FAITH

The writer of Psalm 11 presents us with a penetrating and probing question: "If the foundations are destroyed what can the righteous do?" That is, what must believers do to prevent destruction of the foundation of their faith? The answer to the psalmist's question is found in Jude 3. What will keep the foundations of our faith solid are believers who will take seriously Jude's admonition to "contend earnestly for the faith which was once for all delivered to the saints."

To accomplish that we must go beyond a knowledge of the state of the church and an ability to identify imposters. We must take appropriate and effective action to defend the faith from the destructive work of those imposters.

But how do we defend our faith? Jude, in his epistle, gives us the motivation and the mandate that provide us with the starting point for defending our faith in the face of apostasy.

OUR IRRESISTIBLE MOTIVATION

Jude 3 is an interesting verse. At this point the writer changes topics midstream in his letter. Note Jude's words,

"Beloved, while I was very diligent to write to you concerning our common salvation, I found it necessary to write to you exhorting you to contend earnestly for the faith which was once for all delivered to the saints."

Jude had fully intended to write about "our common salvation." But a compulsion came over him and he changed the direction of his pen. That compulsion was the Holy Spirit moving him to change his message, and Jude was sensitive enough to the Spirit's leading to do so. He was irresistibly motivated.

God's people today need to catch that motivation. For example, the Bible is under attack in our land. We see our universities and seminaries support teachers who do not believe in the historicity of the Bible (e.g., that Adam and Eve were historical people). We make room for those who discount the miracles of the Bible. Rather than stepping out in defense of the faith we are too often content to ignore the problem or compromise with it. Where are God's people today who sense an irresistible motivation to exhort others to "contend earnestly for the faith"?

Jude is speaking about apostasy in an apologetic sense here. He is calling for believers to defend the faith that some are denying; to preserve the faith that some are perverting; and to contend for the faith that some are corrupting. To contend for the faith means that we must take seriously the defense of our most holy faith in days when it is being so subtly undermined.

Why does it seem that so many are sounding the trumpet call today? Because many believers are responding to the irresistible motivation to contend for the faith. Often, we are accused of being intolerant and seeking to gain power when the truth is that we are motivated by an urgency to regain purity of the faith. When, like Jude, we become aware of apostasy, we too will have a compulsion—an irresistible motivation—to contend for the faith.

OUR INESCAPABLE MANDATE

The believer must take seriously the inescapable mandate given the church, which is enveloped in Jude's words "contend earnestly for the faith which was once for all delivered to the saints." An examination of the message of the book of Jude reveals the key aspects of this mandate.

THE CONTENT OF THE MANDATE

What is "the faith"? Whereas "faith" denotes the act of believing, "the faith" is that which is believed. "The faith" is that body of Bible doctrine that makes up the complete revelation of truth. It is the full and final revelation of God contained in the Scriptures. It is the word of truth unfolded from Genesis to Revelation, the Bible.[2] Our mandate is to contend for "the faith" and the content of the mandate is "the faith."

THE COMPLETENESS OF THE MANDATE

Jude says that the mandate is "once for all" delivered to the saints. It was not delivered merely once upon a time, but once for all time! (The Greek word for "once" is properly translated in the *New King James Version* as "once for all").[3] There can be no addition or subtraction. The Bible is a finished work. No wonder the last warning of the Bible sounds the alarm, "For I testify to everyone who hears the words of the prophecy of this book; If anyone adds to these things, God will add to him the plagues that are written in this book; and if anyone takes away from the words of the book of this prophecy, God shall take away his part from the Book of Life, from the holy city, and from the things which are written in this book" (Revelation 22:18-19).

The Bible is complete. It is interesting to note that the

same word used in Jude is used also in Hebrews 9:26-28 to describe our Savior's finished work on the cross. The writer of Hebrews said, "He then would have had to suffer often since the foundation of the world; but now, once at the end of the ages He has appeared to put away sin by the sacrifice of Himself. And as it is appointed for men to die *once*, but after this the judgment, so Christ was offered *once* to bear the sins of many. To those who eagerly wait for Him he will appear a second time, apart from sin, for salvation" (emphasis added). Christ's atonement is complete. Jude uses the same word so that we might see that as the cross is a finished work, so is the Word of God.

The Bible is forever settled in heaven. Someone observed that while astronomers might discover a new star, their discoveries never add to the universe. Before astronomers ever lifted their telescopes to the heavens God had already numbered the stars and named each one. So it is with the Bible. It is ours to study. While we will learn more about it, we can never add to or take anything from it.

One of the clearest indications of apostasy is a distortion of the plain teaching of the Bible. Any claim to further revelation than what is revealed in this Book is evidence of apostasy. The Church of the Latter Day Saints (the Mormon Church) holds to a number of documents it claims are additional revelations from God. The faith which was once for all delivered to the saints does not need a Joseph Smith's Golden Tablet added to it eighteen hundred years later. Paul said, "But even if we, or an angel from heaven, preach any other gospel to you than what we have preached to you, let him be accursed" (Galatians 1:8).

There is not much difference in false believers adding to the Word of God and Christians adding to the Word of God. I have heard some Christians say they have received a "word of prophecy" at a meeting. That "word of prophecy" often directed them to do something diametrically opposed to what has already been revealed in the Word of God. The church has no need for any such "prophecy" today. In comparison, we read in the book of Acts of the New Testament church exercising the gift of prophecy only because it did not have a final, complete written revelation. But we have it today. It is the Bible.

We are living in a day when people add to (extremism) and take away from (liberalism)—and both are wrong. The Bible says it is a clear indication of the last days. This Book of God is the truth, and if we love God we must contend for the faith as long as we have our breath.

THE CUSTODIANS OF THE MANDATE

Jude says the faith is delivered to the "saints." That is, to those who are genuine believers! We have in our care, in our custody, the Word of the living God. That is why we cannot stand idly by and watch this book being ridiculed and torn apart by liberal theologians and false prophets. God has called us to be guardians of His Word.

The word *delivered* in Jude 3 means to "be entrusted with." Paul exhorted young Timothy saying, "The things that you have heard from me among many witnesses, commit these to faithful men who will be able to teach others also" (2 Timothy 2:2). You and I would not have this Word of God today were it not for the faithful down through the centuries who guarded and passed on this precious treasure. When we think of those spiritual forefathers, many of whom gave their lives for this Book, we more clearly see our responsibility to earnestly contend for it today. Perhaps, Isaac Watts said it best when he penned these words:

> Am I a soldier of the cross,
> A follower of the lamb,
> And shall I fear to own his cause
> Or blush to speak his name?

> Must I be carried to the skies
> On flowery beds of ease,
> While others fought to win the prize
> And sailed through bloody seas?

Now the baton has been passed to us. We must hand down this faith to the next generation, uncorrupted and unperverted. That is why we must stand firm in the battle for the Bible today. It is "the Faith"—"once for all delivered"—"to the saints." It was delivered to the saints, not discovered by the saints! It comes from God and not from man, and our responsibility is to contend for it.

THE COMMAND TO CONTEND FOR THE FAITH

We have been delivered a mandate. How are we to defend the faith? Let me suggest four ways.

We must love the faith. This is where we begin our defense. We submit ourselves to the Lord Jesus Christ. Apostates deny him while Christians receive Him. One cannot contend for this faith without loving it in the sense of being saved. Contenders are born-again believers.

We cannot contend for something we do not love. People fight for that which they love. They give their lives for that which they love. Americans have marched off by the hundreds of thousands to fight in wars and conflicts because of their love for liberty. In our fight against apostasy we must do the same. The first step in learning to contend for the faith is to love the Bible, the Word of God. The way to start loving the written Word is to fall in love with the Living Word—Jesus Christ.

We must learn the faith. It is a very difficult thing to defend something we know nothing about. I spent my four undergraduate years at Texas Christian University as a pre-law student. My life's dream (before the Lord called me to the high calling of the ministry) was to be a trial lawyer. I know enough about law to know that a lawyer would do a poor job defending a case he had not studied. And yet there are many believers who say they love the faith and never learn the faith. They never study the Bible, the Word of God.

What do you suppose would happen if the typical preacher in the typical church next Sunday morning asked his parishoners to turn to the book of Hezekiah? Sadly, I fear the majority would start looking for it. (I trust the reader knows it is not there!) Bible illiteracy in the pulpit and in the pew is one of the tragedies of our day. God admonishes us in 2 Timothy 2:15 to study to "present [ourselves] approved to God." If we are students of the Word, we will not be ashamed, for we will be "rightly dividing the word of truth" (v. 15). We are convinced that the Bible is profitable for doctrine, reproof, correction, instruction in righteousness, that the man of God might be complete, thoroughly furnished to every good work (see 3:16). As believers, we should make certain we can give answer in the defense of our faith in three vital areas: (1) the inerrancy of Scripture; (2) the deity of Christ; and (3) salvation by grace through faith. We can never contend for the faith until we learn the faith.

We must live the faith. The final argument for the validity of our faith is not the argument of our lips but the argument of our lives. The greatest argument for Christianity is the life of the believer. Living the faith involves standing unashamedly for the Bible. Not everyone will like us for it. They will consider us narrow-minded. They will accuse us of trying to break the fellowship. When we really live the faith, we should not expect this world, which so viciously crucified our Lord, to take us in with open arms.

All believers should be part of a church that stands for the faith. One way people can live the faith today is by supporting Bible-believing, soul-saving churches. In my early years of ministry I used to tell new converts to attend the church of their choice. I no longer do that. Instead, I tell people to immerse their lives in a Bible-believing, Bible-teaching, soul-saving, disciple-making church.

A serious problem today is that a lot of good people are spinning their wheels in bad churches. How many times have we heard these loyal church members say, "I just hate to leave because our family has been here for so many years. Our children were baptized here thirty years ago. We were married here in the church. Mother's funeral was in the church."

Friend, as a true believer you cannot contend for the faith in an apostate church that has left the truth. Apostate churches do not embrace the Word of God. It is easy to predict that apostate churches, left unchecked, will produce in the next generation a group of young adults who know little about Scripture. Interestingly, apostates are the only people about which the Bible says we should "turn away." I believe those who support the work of apostate churches will one day answer to God for it.

At this point it is important to add that in contending for the faith we must guard against being contentious. Paul admonishes us in Ephesians to "speak the truth in love" (Ephesians 4:15). We are to contend for the faith with a loving spirit. We will fail to contend for the faith if we employ a bitter, hateful, arrogant, or haughty spirit. Far too many Christians speak the truth but do not do so in love. Remember, we live the faith by being Christlike.

As ambassadors of Jesus Christ we speak the truth not only to prove imposters wrong and expose them, but to eventually win them over. The best way I know of winning over people is to speak the truth in love. If I know of someone whose view is contrary to Scripture, I must approach that person in love. Perhaps that person is a babe in Christ and holds a wrong view simply because he has yet to receive proper training, or he has been fooled by false teaching. In any case, you and I need to have a sense of compassion. The Bible says our Lord saw people "as sheep without a shepherd and had compassion for them." We must do no less.

We must loose the faith. We must be about the business of sharing the faith. We often hear people say, "Keep the faith." To the contrary, we are to give it away. The late Paul Little said it best in his classic volume *How to Give Away Your Faith*—if we are not giving our faith away, maybe we should give it up because it may not be real.

THE BELIEVER'S RESPONSIBILITY

All true believers have a responsibility to contend for the faith. Like Jude we should have an irresistible motivation of the Holy Spirit welling up within us. We have an inescapable mandate. How do we contend for the faith, the Word of God delivered to us? By loving the faith, learning the faith, living the faith, and loosing the faith. Unless we become motivated and take seriously this mandate, we will have no one else to blame but ourselves.

ENDNOTES:

1. Samuel Gordon, *Jewels from Jude*. (Belfast: Ambassador Productions, 1985), p. 35.

2. *The Pulpit Commentary*, 23 vols. (New York: Funk and Wagnalls, 1950), 22:4.

3. H. A. Ironside, *The Epistles of John and Jude*. (Neptune, N.J.: Loizeaux, 1931), p. 15.

FIVE

THE DANGERS OF APATHY

The church's major problem in dealing with apostasy today is apathy. Denominations and schools are dying not simply because apostates have crept in, but because genuine believers are apathetic and do little to stem the tide of apostasy in the church.

Jude tells us that we, the church, are prone to apathy. His words in verse 5 indicate this: "I want to remind you, though you once knew this" (v. 5). He calls us to remember. Why? Because we tend to forget! We need only look at our pulpits and pews to see evidence of this.

Webster defines *apathy* as "lacking interest; indifference." In the context of apostasy in the church, it is the church taking a noncommittal position in the face of attack from the enemy. It is the church forfeiting the battle and failing to preserve the integrity of the faith.

Jude gives us a warning against apathy by using three illustrations from history. He relates the experiences of the Israelites, the angels, and the city of Sodom. They all had one thing in common. They fell! Israel lost its victory. The angels lost their vocation. Sodom lost its virtue. Jude's warning is for the church to awaken from its apathy, for it is in danger of losing its victory, its vocation, and its virtue. Perhaps by studying the past we might learn to become overcomers in the future.

THE DANGER OF LOSING OUR VICTORY

"But I want to remind you, though you once knew this, that the Lord, having saved the people out of the land of Egypt, afterward destroyed those who did not believe" (Jude 5).

Shortly after leaving Egyptian bondage and their miraculous passage through the Red Sea, Moses led the Israelites to the very portals of the Promised Land at Kadesh-Barnea. There, he sent twelve spies into the land. Ten of those spies came back with a majority report of giants, walled cities, and no possibility of conquest. The other two spies, Joshua and Caleb, came back with a minority report that, in spite of the truth of the majority report, conveyed the news that the Israelites could conquer the land because God had promised it to them, and He would fight for them. The people voted and the majority report won. The result of that decision was that the Israelites spent the next forty years wandering aimlessly in the wilderness.

Look at the extent of their unbelief. They failed to believe that the same God who had parted the Red Sea, destroyed Pharaoh's army in front of their eyes, provided manna from heaven every morning, led them with a cloud by day and a pillar of fire by night, and poured water from the rock, could also enable them to overcome the land of Canaan, even after He had promised He would. How tragic was their unbelief! They had forgotten what God had done for them. Some of us today are no different. We cannot believe God for the future, yet we have seen Him do so much in the past.

The writer of Hebrews pointedly tells us that Israel lost its victory because of unbelief. He says, "For who, having heard, rebelled? Indeed, was it not all who came out of Egypt, led by Moses? Now with whom was He angry forty years. Was it not with those who sinned, whose corpses fell in the wilderness? And to whom did He swear that they would not enter His rest, but to those who did not obey? So we see that they could not enter in because of unbelief" (Hebrews 3:16-19).

The warning is clear. We run a genuine risk of losing our victory. Jude does not stand alone in Scripture with his warning to believers who fall into unbelief. The Christian can become what the apostle Paul called a "castaway." That is, he will receive no crown in heaven, but will be saved though as by fire. John tells us that there is a sin unto death that believers can commit. "If anyone sees his brother sinning a sin which does not lead to death, he will ask, and He will give him life for those who commit sin not leading to death. There is sin leading to death. I do not say that he should pray about that" (1 John 5:16). Ananias and Sapphira are examples of the sin unto death (Acts 5:1-11).

We can benefit from the experience of the children of Israel. Paul says, "These things happened to them as examples, and they were written for our admonition on whom the ends of the ages have come" (1 Corinthians 10:11). The great lesson here is that even though God has saved us, He reserves the right to discipline us if we become guilty of unbelief, and the sin to which it leads.[1] God can and will take away the victory of those who think they can go on in sin and get away with it. Jude warns against the danger of losing our victory. Remember the Israelites! Their unbelief took away their victory.

THE DANGER OF LOSING OUR VOCATION

"And the angels who did not keep their proper domain, but left their own abode, He has reserved in everlasting chains under darkness for the judgment of the great day" (Jude 6).

This passage refers to angels who lost their position, their vocation. The angels had sinned against God. The nature of their sin was "in a similar manner as the sin of Sodom"—sexual perversion. They went after "different flesh."[2]

To what extent was the sin of those angels like the sin of Sodom? I am convinced he is referring to an experience that happened back in the days before the Flood. The Bible records:

> Now it came to pass, when men began to multiply on the face of the earth, and daughters were born to them, that the sons of God saw the daughters of men, that they were beautiful; and they took wives for themselves of all whom they chose. And the Lord said, My spirit shall not strive with man forever, for he is indeed flesh; yet his days shall be one hundred and twenty years. There were giants on the earth in those days and also afterward, when the sons of God came in to the daughters of men, and they bore children to them. Those were the mighty men who were of old, men of renown. [Genesis 6:1-4]

The term "sons of God" is translated "angels" in the Septuagint (the Greek translation of the original Hebrew text). Also, the Hebrew rendering "sons of God" is used exclusively of angels in the Old Testament. What we can best understand from these verses is that some of the fallen angels came to earth during the days of Noah and had sexual relations with women, thus producing a race of giants which the Bible refers to as the *nephilim*. This sin was one of the reasons God destroyed the world by the Flood. By their own volition these angelic creatures rebelled against God and left their lofty positions, and in leaving, lost their vocation.

Two things brought about the downfall of these angels. First, their pride caused them to fall. They wanted to "be like the most high God." Second, they were lustful. Where pride and lust rule, vocation is sacrificed. The doom of those fallen angels is sealed. They have lost their vocation and cut themselves off from everything that might have been theirs. They lost it all through unbelief and pride.[3] The church needs to heed Jude's warning lest it meet a similar fate.

So what is the church doing today? By and large, it is sitting in its apathy—in spite of the warnings of Scripture. Many men and women today have lost their privileges as believers and their position of service because of their pride and lust. The church can no longer afford to remain in its apathy. It must heed Jude's call to "wake up and remember!"

THE DANGER OF LOSING OUR VIRTUE

"Sodom and Gomorrah, and the cities around them in a similar manner to these, having given themselves over to sexual immorality and gone after strange flesh, are set forth as an example, suffering the vengeance of eternal fire" (Jude 7).

The account about which Jude speaks is recorded in Genesis 19. Angelic visitors came to visit Lot. They evidently came in human form. Lot took them into his home for the night, but a crowd soon gathered outside so that they might engage in homosexual acts with the visitors. In a vain attempt to defuse the situation, Lot offered his two virgin daughters to the crowd. It is shocking to read in Genesis 19:8 that Lot offered his own daughters to these perverted men. However, the crowd did not want female companionship; all they could think of was having sex with these men. As the story unfolds, they were struck with blindness, but even that didn't stop them. They continued to grope in the dark for the door handle to get to these celestial visitors.

No wonder Jude sounds the warning "Remember Sodom!" When man goes too far, God gives him over. Paul alluded to this in Romans 1 when he said:

Professing to be wise, they became fools, and changed the glory of the incorruptible God into an image made like corruptible man—and birds and four-footed animals and creeping things. Therefore God also gave them up to uncleanness, in the lusts of their hearts, to dishonor their bodies among themselves, who exchanged the truth of God for the lie, and worshiped and served the creature rather than the Creator, who is blessed forever. Amen.

For this reason, God gave them up to vile passions. For even their women exchanged the natural use for what is against nature. Likewise also the men, leaving the natural use of the woman, burned in their lust for one another, men with men committing what is shameful, and receiving in themselves the penalty of their error which was due. And even as they did not like to retain God in their knowledge, God gave them over to a debased mind, to do those things which are not fitting. [Romans 1:22-28]

Christ Himself prophesied that the last days would be as the days of Lot when He said, "Likewise as it was also in the days of Lot: They ate, they drank, they bought, they sold, they planted, they built; but on the day that Lot went out of Sodom it rained fire and brimstone from heaven and destroyed them all. Even so, will it be in the day when the Son of Man is revealed" (Luke 17:28-30).

Be assured that God does not sit by idly, smiling at our sin. He "rained fire and brimstone on Sodom and Gomorrah" and "overthrew those cities" (Genesis 19:24-25). Nearly two thousand years have passed since Jude warned us to "Remember Sodom!" and today countless unbelievers go right on ignoring that warning. However, we need to remember that these words were not written to unbelievers, but to those who are believers, those who have been "called" by God, who are "beloved" by the Father, and "kept" by the Lord Jesus Christ. These things were written so that we might not lose our virture.

THE CHURCH'S ONLY HOPE

If we ignore the words of Jude, there is no hope for the church. This should make every Christian an earnest soul-winner and a defender of the faith. What the Bible says God did to the Israelites, the angels, and the Sodomites, He can and possibly will do again! Why should we think we are going to sin and get away with it? The evangelist Billy Graham, in commenting on that state of the American church, said, "If God doesn't punish America, he will have to apologize to Sodom and Gomorrah."[4]

The fabric of our society is unraveling before our very eyes. In the fall of 1986 we read the report of the Attorney General's Commission on Pornography in America. Under the protection of so-called First Amendment rights, we are seeing in our nation today what would make the inhabitants of Sodom blush. James Dobson, president of Focus on the Family and a member of the Commission, reports that "the mainstream of explicit material sold in sex shops today focuses on rape, incest, defecation, urination, mutilation, beastiality, vomiting, enemas, homosexuality, and sado-masochistic activity."[5] Although we might be justified in pointing an accusing finger at Sodom, this is America about which we are speaking! And by and large, the American church tragically sits by and watches in total apathy.

The church appears to have given up without a fight. We have been infiltrated by imposters in the classroom and pulpit. These synthetic saints, under the guise of being true believers, have turned the grace of God into lewdness. And we have allowed them to rock us into a sleep of apathy.

Israel's sin was unbelief. The angels' sin was rebellion against authority. Sodom's sin was sensual indulgence. Those are the three sins that characterize apostates. They do not live by faith, they reject authority, and they cannot control their sensual passions. Consequently, they creep into churches and schools and try to fool true believers.

It is time for preachers today to stand in the pulpit and preach the Word fearlessly and faithfully. It's time for us to awaken from our apathy and to remember the Israelites, to remember the angels, and to remember Sodom—lest we lose our victory, our vocation, and our virtue.

ENDNOTES:

1. Maxwell Coder, *Jude: the Acts of the Apostates* (Chicago: Moody, 1958), p. 27.

2. J. N. Kelly, *A Commentary on the Epistle of Peter and Jude* (Grand Rapids: Baker, 1969), p. 258.

3. William Barclay, *The Letters of John and Jude* (Philadelphia: Westminster Press, 1958), p. 216.

4. Samuel Gordon, *Jewels from Jude* (Belfast: Ambassador Productions, 1985), p. 71.

5. Report of Attorney General's Commission on Pornography in America.

SIX

SOUNDING THE ALARM

The church's position in the ecclesiastical world today is that of impending judgment. I am convinced that only a genuine spiritual awakening, a fresh new wind of the Holy Spirit, can avert the judgment of God upon the apostasy of our nation and world.

The book of Jude predicts what will happen in the latter days of the Church Age. In fact, Jude seems to be writing about the very days in which we are living! Jude's purpose in prophesying is to encourage the church to discern apostasy when it raises its devisive and destructive head so that it might "earnestly contend for the faith."

It is clear that because Satan has not succeeded in destroying the church from without through persecution, he is now at work to destroy it from within by means of apostasy in the pulpit and apathy in the pew. Satan is not fighting the church today—he is joining it!

Jude is sounding the alarm for us by prophesying that, in these latter days, apostates will go the way of Cain, who perverted the mode of worship, the way of Balaam, who perverted the motive of worship, and the way of Korah, who perverted the manner of worship. Certainly, we as believers of the church of Jesus Christ cannot afford to ignore Jude's message.

When our daughters were little they enjoyed riding their bicycles. Whenever they went out the front door of our home to ride their bikes, I would say, "Don't ride your bicycles in the street!" After each little speech would come the same reply, "We know, Daddy! How many times do you have to tell us?" As parents know, those kinds of warnings must be repeated so they will sink in and become part of a child's thoughts and actions.

The same principle applies to the warnings of the book of Jude. Jude chose to repeat his warnings in various modes so they would sink into our minds. The apostle Paul also practiced repetition in his epistles. He said, "Finally, my brethren, rejoice in the Lord. For me to write the same things to you is not tedious, but for you it is safe" (Philippians 3:1).

As Jude views apostasy in a prophetic sense, he describes the characteristics of apostates and the nature of their activities. While it is true that every apostate might not possess every characteristic, it is true that all apostates will have some of the characteristics and be actively involved in some of the destructive activities outlined in Jude 8-11.

Jude prophesied that in the last days apostates would do two things. First, they will pollute the witness of the church. They will do this in body by defiling the flesh, that is, by immorality; they will do this in soul, by being insubordinate, that is, they will "reject authority"; they will do this in spirit by being irreverent, that is, they will "speak evil of dignitaries." Second, he says they will pervert the worship of Christ in mode, motive, and manner. Let's look at the first activity.

Apostates Will Pollute the Witness of the Church

Likewise also these dreamers defile the flesh, reject authority, and speak evil of dignitaries. Yet Michael the archangel, in contending with the devil, when he disputed about the body of Moses, dared not bring against him a reviling accusation, but said, 'The Lord rebuke you!' But these speak evil of whatever they do not know; and whatever they know naturally, like brute beasts, in these things they corrupt themselves. [Jude 8-10]

Apostates pollute the witness of the church with every fiber of their being. Man is trichotomous, which means he is made of three parts—body, soul, and spirit. Those elements make up his real identity. Although he lives in a body, the real man is that which lives as long as God lives—his spirit. Apostates pollute the church with body, soul, and spirit.

Jude tells us that apostates are "dreamers" (verse 8). They live in an unreal dream world. They bought into the lie Satan first used in the Garden of Eden when he said to the Eve, "You shall be like God" (Genesis 2:5). Jude says of apostates, "But these speak evil of whatever they do not know; and whatever they know naturally, like brute beasts in these things they corrupt themselves" (verse 10).

Immoral actions that would have been openly rebuked in pulpits just a generation ago are today accepted in many of those same pulpits. "Dreamers" are rocking to sleep their congregations while helping them to feel comfortable in their sin. When preachers pollute their pulpits by discounting such crucial doctrines as the infallibility and inerrancy of the Word of God, it is not long before their moral code goes along with it—body, soul, and spirit.

Apostates Will Be Immoral

After rejecting truth, apostates often have a tendency to become involved in sensual sin. And sooner or later most false teachers are exposed on a moral level. Jim Jones was recognized by the citizens of San Francisco as a religious leader. We all know of the tragedy at Jonestown, Guyana.

On the surface Jones's organization appeared to be filled with love. But appearances can be deceiving. Jones and his followers defiled the flesh and, as we all know, destroyed the flesh.

Apostasy and defilement of the flesh are Siamese twins, and they are linked together in Scripture. The apostle Peter said,

> For if, after they have escaped the pollutions of the world through the knowledge of the Lord and Savior Jesus Christ, they are again entangled in them and overcome, the latter end is worse for them than the beginning. For it would have been better for them not to have known the way of righteousness, than having known it, to turn from the holy commandment delivered to them. [2 Peter 2:20-21]

The new morality we hear about is nothing more than the old immorality. People making light of marriage vows, living in open adultery, joining homosexual clubs and bathhouses are not new concepts. Jude prophesied more than 1900 years ago that these kinds of things would signal the age of apostasy.

Here's a word of caution. As we seek to heed Jude's warnings against imposters, we must be careful not to judge others too quickly. Because one falls into sin does not automatically signify that that person is an apostate. Before we don our ecclesiastical garments and look down our noses at anyone else, we need to remind ourselves of 1 Corinthians 10:12: "Let him who thinks he stands take heed, lest he fall."

APOSTATES WILL BE INSUBORDINATE

In the well-known Great Commission passage Jesus said, "All authority has been given to me in heaven and on earth" (Matthew 28:18). The word "authority" is the Greek word *exousia*, which means "right" or "authority." If Jesus has *all* authority, Satan has none. The only authority he has over our lives is what we allow him.

All authority originates with God.[1] Whether it be the authority of the home, the church, or government, it has its source in Him. He has established those institutions to be guardians of His authority and to carry out His will.

Rejecting the authority God has established is dangerous business indeed. In spite of that, many people today flat out reject God's authority. Jude tells us that an apostate is subordinate in his soul. Emotionally, by an act of his will, he rejects it.

AUTHORITY OF THE HOME

God instituted the authority of the home. Should we be surprised that many leaders of the feminist movement do not pay heed to the teachings of the Bible on the authority of the home? Even worse, liberal theologians who support the modern feminist movement neglect and reject the teaching of authority in the home found in Ephesians 5.

AUTHORITY OF THE CHURCH

The Bible is our sole authority for rule and faith. Should we be surprised that leaders of dying denominations and churches do not hold to the inerrancy of Scripture? Today we see imposters in our churches and schools undermining the Bible—our infallible, inerrant, authoritative rule of faith. They attack the Bible because it represents God's authority.

AUTHORITY OF GOVERNMENT

Apostasy in the church has been on the rise since the turn of the century. Since then we have seen a serious and orchestrated attempt to undo the authority of government our forefathers established.

Apostate religious leaders are often associated with subversive organizations, especially in Third World countries. Should we be surprised that leftist regimes that undermine governments scoff at the Bible as irrelevant? It is interesting that often rejection of the authority of the Bible goes hand in hand with a demand for a new social order.

Of course, we know that the underlying reason apostates reject authority is that they reject the Lord Jesus Christ and His rule over their lives. They do not want a God who rules over them. They refuse to be boxed in by any parameters. Those who have fallen away from the faith take the precious Bible doctrine of the priesthood of the believer and pervert it to make it a license to believe anything they wish.

APOSTATES WILL BE IRREVERENT

If it is true that these people who have fallen away from the faith are immoral in body and insubordinate in soul, it is not surprising that they are also irreverent in spirit. Jude says that apostates "speak evil of dignitaries" (verse 8). The word Jude uses in this verse for "dignitaries" is the Greek word *doxa*. It literally means "glorious ones."

The apostate is irreverent in spirit toward the things of God, which is borne out by his cynicism, ridicule, and blasphemy. The phrase *speak evil* literally means "to blaspheme." We are not simply talking about taking the Lord's name in vain. To speak evil of dignitaries means to deliberately take God's Word lightly and make light of His created beings.

The apostle John, exiled to the Island of Patmos as an old man, addressed the pastors of the seven churches of Asia in the book of Revelation by referring to them as "angels." The *Century Bible* suggests that the phrase *speak evil of dignitaries* refers to the "constituted authorities of the church." In other words, when apostates speak evil of dignitaries, they do so of God's appointed and anointed leadership.

This spirit of cynicism and accusation comes from Satan himself. One of the titles the Bible gives him is the "accuser of the brethren" (Revelation 12:10). Christians fall into Satan's trap and do his work when they "speak evil" of each other, and especially of those God has placed in positions of authority.

It is bad enough that the ungodly, who represent an evil cause, speak evil of the authority of God and His church. The apostle Paul urges the believer to "speak evil of no one" (Titus 3:2). Contending for the faith is one thing, but we are never to be contentious in doing so.

Immorality, insubordination, and irreverence have their result. As Jude puts it, apostates "like brute beasts, in these things they corrupt themselves" (verse 10). In a sense apostates are like animals. They live solely by natural instinct. They criticize what they do not understand and destroy themselves in the process.[2] There is nothing spiritual about them. Professing to be wise, they become fools.

The spirit of apostasy pollutes the witness of the church. Looking around us today we wonder if the complete fulfillment of Jude's prophecy is near. Never before have we heard so many speaking evil of dignitaries. Moses' authorship of the Pentateuch is openly scoffed at even though the Lord Jesus Himself affirmed it. We are living in a theological environment today in which men and institutions truly adhering to the inerrancy of Scripture are attacked and accused of all manner of evil. In many ways Jude's prophecy is being fulfilled.

APOSTATES WILL PERVERT THE WORSHIP OF CHRIST

God pronounces a "woe" upon those guilty of apostasy. In Jude 11 we read, "Woe to them! For they have gone in the way of Cain, have run greedily in the error of Balaam for profit, and perished in the rebellion of Korah." In the Greek language of the New Testament a woe was used to denote a culmination or calamity. It was a word of hopelessness and sorrow.

So we see our Lord pronouncing a woe upon those who pervert the worship of Christ in mode, motive, and manner. What an example to those of us who minister of God to the church. Our gospel message needs to be balanced with the warning of coming judgment.

THE MODE OF WORSHIP PERVERTED

Jude tells us that apostates go "the way of Cain." What is the way of Cain? We find the answer in Genesis 4:1-7:

> Now Adam knew Eve his wife, and she conceived and bore Cain, and said, I have acquired a man from the Lord. Then she bore again, this time his brother Abel. Now Abel was a keeper of sheep, but Cain was a tiller of the ground. And in the process of time it came to pass that Cain brought an offering of the fruit of the ground to the Lord. Abel also brought of the firstborn of his flock and of their fat. And the Lord respected Abel and his offering, but he did not respect Cain and his offering. And Cain was very angry, and his countenance fell. So the Lord said to Cain, "Why are you angry? And why has your countenance fallen? If you do well, will you not be accepted? And if you do not do well, sin lies at the door. And its desire is for you, but you should rule over it."

On the surface that might seem unfair. Abel brought a sacrifice—a lamb—and shed the blood of that lamb as offering to God. Why did God have respect for his offering? Because "without shedding of blood there is no remission" (Hebrews 9:22). Sin is not forgiven without the shedding of blood. Abel's lamb was a picture of the blood of Christ on the cross of Calvary. John writes in 1 John 1:7: "The blood of

Jesus Christ His Son cleanses us from all sin."

In contrast to Abel's sacrifice, Cain brought an offering of the works of his hands. He brought the ripest grain and the best of his crop. In addition, he was a good man and a hard worker. Shouldn't God have accepted his offering? That is the reasoning of those who pervert the mode of worship. They have gone the way of Cain.

In today's language, the way of Cain is the way of good works. Cain was the first apostate. He knew the way of worship was through the blood of the sacrifice by faith, but he fell from that. He attempted to approach God without the blood of a substitute; instead, he offered the work of his own hands. In doing so, he perverted the mode of worship.

Abel, on the other hand, offered his sacrifice *by faith*. Hebrews 11:4 reads: "By faith Abel offered to God a more excellent sacrifice than Cain, through which he obtained witness that he was righteous, God testifying of his gifts; and through it he being dead still speaks." Faith is believing what God says. But Cain set aside the word of God. His religion was based primarily on good works.

We see the tragedy of Cain today. How many reject the way of substitutionary atonement and, being too proud to admit their need of a substitute, offer the very best of their own efforts. Sadly, the Bible records, "Cain went out from the presence of the Lord" (Genesis 4:16). That is the plight of many today who go the way of Cain and pervert the mode of worship. The Bible reminds us that, "For by grace you have been saved through faith, and that not of yourselves; it is the gift of God, not of works, lest anyone should boast" (Ephesians 2:8-9).

One of the sure signs of an apostate is his neglect of emphasis on the vicarious death of our Lord Jesus Christ and His shed blood as an atonement for our sin. The apostate does not teach or preach about the blood of Christ.

Certainly, one would not expect to find professors in Christian schools and seminaries teaching this perversion of worship. Yet, with a broken heart, we know that some semi-naries today are teaching our young preachers that vicar-ious punishment is neither meaningful nor moral.

Let's call an Old Testament witness to the stand to testify about this matter. Let's ask Isaiah what he thinks about the blood atonement and the substitutionary death of Christ. We hear him reply, "But He was wounded for our transgressions, He was bruised for our iniquities; the chas-tisement for our peace was upon Him, and by His stripes we are healed. All we like sheep have gone astray; we have turned, every one, to his own way; and the Lord has laid on Him the iniquity of us all" (Isaiah 53:5-6).

Now let's call a New Testament witness to the stand and see what he says about the substitutionary death of Christ. Let's ask the apostle Paul what he says about the blood atonement. Hear him reply, "For I delivered to you first of all that which I also received: that Christ died for our sins according to the Scriptures" (1 Corinthians 15:3). We can thank God for the vicarious, substitutionary death of the Lord Jesus Christ on the cross. God have mercy on those who discount it!

There are only two kinds of religion in the world: true religion and false religion. True religion is represented by Abel and the blood, and false religion is represented by Cain and all others who try to get to heaven by their own good works. Solomon summed up well the way of Cain when he said, "There is a way that seems right to a man, but its end is the way of death" (Proverbs 16:25).

I am amazed at how many people are regular church-goers but go the way of Cain. In some churches in our land are people who sit in their pews week after week but never hear a message on the blood of Christ or the fact that Christ died as a substitute for our sins. The result is that these churches are raising a generation of children who will know nothing of the necessity of the cross. For them the cross will carry no urgency; it will simply be a sentimental story.

Charles Hadden Spurgeon said it best, "The true test of whether a man is preaching the Gospel or not, is the emphasis he places on the blood of Christ."

THE MOTIVE OF WORSHIP PERVERTED

What should be our motive for worship? It should be to meet God and glorify Him. Yet, Jude tells us that apostates "run greedily in the error of Balaam for profit" (v. 11). What is the error of Balaam? We find his story in Numbers 22-24. The Israelites had camped in the plains of Moab near the Jordan River across from Jericho. Their presence intimidated King Balak, so he tried to bribe a Gentile prophet, Balaam, to curse the Israelites. But Balaam refused and went away. However, the more he thought about the offer the greedier his heart became. So Balaam returned with a plan (with a fee, of course!) to cause God to curse the Israelites. He arranged a sensual feast in which a number of Israelite boys attended. It wasn't long before fornication took over and the curse of God came upon His people, resulting in the tragic judgment of death for 24,000.

The error of Balaam was using spiritual motives for material gain. And his error was not just doing what he did, but also in thinking he could get away with it. Balaam was in religion for what he could get out of it.

Originally Balaam sought to please God. But along the way he also decided to please man and himself at the same time. Our Lord warned against this error, "No one can serve two masters; for either he will hate the one and love the other, or else he will be loyal to the one and despise the other. You cannot serve God and mammon" (Matthew 6:24).

The apostle Peter also addressed this issue of true motive of worship,

But there were also false prophets among the people, even as there will be false teachers among you, who will secretly bring in destructive heresies, even denying the Lord who bought them, and bring on themselves swift destruction. And many will follow their destructive ways, because of whom the way of truth will be blasphemed. By covetousness they will exploit you with deceptive words; for a long time their judgment has not been idle, and their destruction does not slumber. [2 Peter 2:1-3]

According to the Bible, apostates are filled with covetousness and generally motivated by money. Paul said they are "lovers of pleasure rather than lovers of God" (2 Timothy 3:4). For some, the motive is contacts. Some join certain churches to make key business contacts. It is not wrong for Christians to do business with each other as long as their motives are pure. But woe unto those who pervert the motive of worship by running "greedily in the error of Balaam for profit."

We see the tragedy of Balaam today. Many stifle their own convictions for temporary gain. Others alter their message to gain certain advantages. Those who do so are guilty of compromise.

The message of Scripture is that those who serve the Lord are not to be in it for the money or to gain advantage. The believer's sole motive for worship is to glorify God.

THE MANNER OF WORSHIP PERVERTED

The manner of true worship is to do everything decently and in order. The apostle Paul said, "Let nothing be done through selfish ambition or conceit, but in lowliness of mind let each esteem others better than himself" (Philippians 2:3). He also said that as believers we are to submit "to one another in the fear of God" (Ephesians 5:21).

Jude likens apostates to "the rebellion of Korah." Korah's story is found in Numbers 16. It was he who led a revolt against the leadership of Moses (God's prophet) and

Aaron (God's priest). Korah was a Levite who, lured by pride, formed a conspiracy with three other men and led two hundred of Israel's elders in a rebellion against God's appointed leaders. Korah did not want to submit to Moses' leadership and authority. He was too blind to see that in opposing Moses and Aaron, he was opposing God. As a result Korah perverted the manner of worship because he had a problem with authority.

God responded to the rebellion of Korah with fire. He answered by fire. God brought about a swift judgment on Korah and his followers (see Numbers 16:31-35). The Bible simply says that they perished.

The word "rebellion" in Jude 11 is from the Greek word *antilogia*, which means "against the word." Whereas Cain ignored the word of God and Balaam opposed the word of God, Korah rebelled against the word of God. Such is the progression of the apostate. He begins by simply ignoring what the Bible says. Then he moves into opposing it by holding that the Bible is not the Word of God. Once he reaches that point, it is not long before he openly rebels against God's holy Word.

In our churches are men and women who refuse to be under authority, who like Korah, gather groups about them to oppose God's anointed and appointed. Only God knows how many churches have split because of the spirit of apostasy that caused men and women to perish in "the rebellion of Korah."

The warning here is that when we speak unjustly against God's anointed and appointed, we speak against the Lord Himself, who is the bestower of all authority. Paul sounded the warning in his epistle to Titus when he said, "Remind them to be subject to rulers and authorities, to obey, to be ready for every good work, to speak evil of no one, to be peaceable, gentle, showing all humility to all men" (Titus 3:1-2).

In Jude 11 we get a vivid picture of the plight of the

apostate. Note the tenses of the verbs in this verse: "have gone, have run, perished." The apostate goes down the wrong road, and before long, finds himself running down that road until he finally destroys himself.

JUDE'S PROPHECY

Jude's look at apostasy is coming true today. Apostates are polluting the witness of the church in body, soul, and spirit. Their activities—immorality, insubordination, and irreverence—are clearly evident. It is as though Jude were alive today and writing to us in the morning newspaper.

This prophetic warning should cause each of us to ask himself two questions. First, What about my witness? Is it polluted or clean? Second, What about my worship? Is it perverted or clear? True believers who keep silent and compromise to avoid conflict and confrontation will be held responsible for not contending for the faith.

According to God's Word, the danger of apostasy is to know the will of God and not act upon it. We all need to learn from the accounts of these three men in Jude 11. Fearful judgments await those who know the truth and reject it.

ENDNOTES:

1. Warren Wiersbe, *Be Alert* (Wheaton, Ill: Victor Books, 1984), p. 144.

2. William Barclay, *The Letters of John and Jude* (Philadelphia: Westminster, 1958), p. 221.

SEVEN

SAFEGUARDING AGAINST IMPOSTERS

As we consider the sea of apostasy around us and the effectiveness of imposter activity in today's church, it seems as though the church has little hope in stemming the tide. However, according to the book of Jude, not only can we stem the tide, we can take positive action to deal directly with imposters.

> But you, beloved, remember the words which were spoken before by the apostles of our Lord Jesus Christ: how they told you that there would be mockers in the last time who would walk according to their own ungodly lusts. These are sensual persons, who cause divisions, not having the Spirit. But you, beloved, building yourselves up on your most holy faith, praying in the Holy spirit, keep yourselves in the love of God, looking for the mercy of our Lord Jesus Christ unto eternal life. And on some have compassion, making a distinction; but others save with fear, pulling them out of the fire, hating even the garment defiled by the flesh. [Jude 17-23]

What can we do about imposters? Note that Jude begins verse 17 with the word *but*. This word signals a reversal. The message is that the church can have an impact on apostasy. It can effectively deal with imposters. Jude goes on to give us three important keys to survival in these days of apostasy. He calls on all true believers to be educated, insulated, and separated.

Compassion is the believer's trademark in dealing with imposters. Jude admonishes us, as followers of Jesus Christ, to have compassion for imposters as we defend our faith.

What should be our response to the apostasy of our day? How must we deal with apostasy and the work of imposters? First, we need to be educated as to who the apostate is, what he does, and why he does it. Second, we need to be insulated by keeping ourselves in the love of God. Finally, we need to be separated with a warm, living sacrifice that bears witness in a compassionate, courageous, and cautious way to those without Christ.

BE EDUCATED

Every true believer should be educated regarding three crucial questions about apostates: who? what? and why? We need to know who they are. We need to know what they do. And we need to know why they do what they do.

Initially, we need to be educated as to *who* apostates are. Jude tells us they are "mockers . . . who would walk according to their own ungodly lusts" (v. 18). Today some in our classrooms are saying, "Well, perhaps the Bible is not the inerrant, trustworthy, and infallible revelation of God after all." Many discredit it and claim that it is not true. Others say that it contains the Word of God but that it is not really the Word of God. The irony is that every professor who denies the inerrancy of Scripture is proving, in a sense, its claim to inerrancy. We can expect in the last days attacks on the Bible.

This word *mocker* is an interesting word in the Greek language. It means to "act in a childish fashion, to be childish, to play." There is a world of difference in being childish and childlike. Our Lord said that if anyone would come after Him, he must come as a little child. The Lord honors childlikeness but abhors childishness.

In dealing with apostasy in a sympathetic sense, we must be educated as to who the apostate really is. He is childish in his behavior because he is a "mocker." Apostates mock at the gospel. This certainly is not novel. We should not be surprised if we are mocked, for our Lord was mocked. To me the most heartbreaking aspect of our Lord's cross experience is not the physical brutality to which He was subjected. Rather, that they stripped Him naked, put on Him a scarlet robe, plaited a crown of thorns and pressed it upon His brow, then bowed in front of Him and "mocked" Him. They laughed. A mocker is one who treats the Word (living or written) in open defiance! Those who mock Scripture today are no different from those who mocked the living Word Himself.

A final insight into the character of the mocker. He walks after his "own ungodly lusts" (Jude 18). He is a slave to sin and to self, which explains why he denies the truth. He does not want a God who tells him how to live. Peter talked about mockers in the last days when he said, "Knowing this first: that scoffers will come in the last days, walking according to their own lusts" (2 Peter 3:3).

We also need to be educated as to *what* the apostate does. If by now the reader has not been able to distinguish an apostate believer from an authentic believer, we have one more description. They are sensual persons who cause divisions (see v. 19).

First, they are sensual in their behavior. Again we see apostasy and sensual sins linked together in Scripture. The word *sensual* comes from the Greek *psychikos*. It means "limited to the senses, limited to the soul."[1] Man is made up of spirit, soul, and body, and it is the spirit part of him that communes with God. The unsaved person, who is dead spiritually, can only operate on a "soulish" level. Nothing about him is spiritual. He operates and makes decisions solely on the basis of his own selfish ambitions and desires (see v. 18).

One of the tragedies of today's superficial Christianity is that many cannot discern between spiritual ministries and soulish ministries. Spiritual ministries edify; while soulish ministries entertain. Spiritual ministries seek the applause and amen of God, while soulish ministries seek the applause and amen of men. Synthentic saints can only function in the soulish realm. In Jude's words they "not having the Spirit" (v. 19).

Second, imposters cause divisions. I have noticed in the current battle for the Bible that when someone believes the Bible is "truth, without any mixture of error" and rises up against the apostasy of his day, he is usually labeled a trouble-maker and called divisive. But it is not the Bible believers that are causing division. Jude says it is the apostate who causes division.

Division is common in days of apostasy. In recent years we have seen divisions in the Presbyterian and Lutheran churches. True believers, who in good conscience can no longer support apostate teachings, have had to establish new churches and, in some cases, even new denominations to preserve the truth for posterity. Apostates can lay the blame on others with accusations of narrow-mindedness and intolerance until they are blue in the face, but the Bible is crystal-clear in its revelation that it is the apostate who is guilty.

Jude tells us that we need to be educated as to *why* apostates do what they do. Verse 19 informs us that they have not the Spirit. That is, they simply do not have the Holy Spirit resident within. That explains why they can be immoral in body, insubordinate in soul, and irreverent in spirit. Is it no wonder they are sensual, that they cause division? That they walk according to their own ungodly lusts?

Since God is not resident in the apostate's life, nothing

about this imposter is spiritual. It soon becomes blatantly obvious that no matter how much the apostate professes with his lips, he is not an authentic believer. Paul emphasizes this point. "If anyone does not have the Spirit of Christ, he is not His" (Romans 8:9).

The residence of God is what makes the difference between the synthetic and the sincere saint. How thankful we should be as true believers that "God has sent forth the Spirit of His Son into your hearts" (Galatians 4:6). No wonder Paul said, "Christ in you, the hope of glory" (Colossians 1:27).

BE INSULATED

It is not enough simply to be educated; we must also safeguard ourselves by insulation. What is our insulation in days of apostasy? Jude says, "Keep yourselves in the love of God" (v. 21). Our Lord referred to this the evening before the crucifixion when He admonished us saying, "Abide in My love" (John 15:9). We are to keep ourselves in the love of God, which is our protection against the activities of imposters. Note that Jude did not say, "Keep on loving God." It is not our love for Him but His love for us that is at issue here.

As true believers we can know that love. Paul revealed in Ephesians that he wanted us to know the love of Christ that surpasses knowledge and gave us four ways by which to do so. He referred to the "width and length and depth and height of God's love" (3:18). (1) The breadth of His love is seen in the fact that "God so loved the world that He gave His only begotten Son, that whoever believes in Him shall not perish but have everlasting life" (John 3:16). God loves everyone. (2) The length of His love is seen in the fact that none of us can sin ourselves out of the love of God; He just keeps on loving us. (3) The depth of His love is seen in the fact that He came down, past solar systems and constellations to become helpless as a tiny seed planted in the virgin's womb. He then demonstrated His own love toward us in that "while we were still sinners, Christ died for us." (4) The height of His love is seen in the fact that He has raised us to sit in the heavenlies in Christ Jesus. It is in this love that we are to "keep ourselves."

Note that Jude's admonition is to "keep yourselves." That places a burden on us. While it is true that he "keeps us from stumbling" on the divine side, there is also a human side. We are to keep ourselves in His love. The best illustration of this is found in Luke 15 in the well-known story of the Prodigal Son. Here was a lad who took his inheritance and left the comfort and protection of his father's love to journey into the "far country." Once there, he wasted all he had on wild living and ended up in a pigpen longing for the husks of corn that the pigs were eating. All the while the loving and patient father awaited the day when the prodigal would return. We all know the happy ending with its reconciliation and rejoicing.

The point is simple. When the prodigal left home it did not mean that his father stopped loving him. But, it did mean he had gotten himself outside of the environment of that love. All the while the son was away, the father's love for him never changed! What had changed was that the boy had removed himself from the place of blessing and the benefit of the father's love.[3] And so it is with us. We can know nothing of His love when we are in the "far country." Many of us have removed ourselves from the place of blessing and love and are no longer "abiding in the love of God." When the prodigal returned home he once again experienced the father's love. The same can be true for us. To "keep ourselves in the love of God" is to stay in His will and be what He wants us to be and where He wants us to be.

The secret of staying in His love is wrapped up in three important words in Jude 20-21: building, praying, looking. These words are participles describing how we are to keep ourselves in the love of God.[3] First is an inward look of edification; "building yourselves up on your most holy faith." Second, is an upward look of supplication; "praying in the Holy Spirit." Third, is a forward look of anticipation; "looking for the mercy of our Lord Jesus Christ unto eternal life." The way to keep ourselves in the Father's love is to build ourselves in the Word of God, pray in the Holy Spirit, and keep on looking for Jesus!

The inward look of edification. Jude 20 is clear; we are to be "building [ourselves] on [our] most holy faith." That *most holy faith* is the same thing as "the faith"—the complete body of Bible doctrine that makes up the perfect whole of truth. It is the Bible! (Remember, "faith" is the act of believing whereas "the faith" is that which is believed.) We are to stay insulated by keeping ourselves in the love of Christ, and the first step in doing this is to build our faith upon the Word of God.

The more we build up ourselves, the better insulated we will be from the effects of apostasy. Scripture is powerful. In his letter to a young preacher boy, the apostle Paul said, "All Scripture is given by inspiration of God, and is profitable for doctrine, for reproof, for correction, for instruction in righteousness, that the man of God may be complete, thoroughly equipped for every good work" (2 Timothy 3:16-17).

Just a word about feeding ourselves on the Word of God. The only way we can build up ourselves is to get in the Word of God. I know people who study the Bible, and I know people who know people who study the Bible. If all we get out of the Bible is what someone else has discovered for himself, we'll never build up *ourselves* in the Word. Unfortunately, too many Christians today are reading books about the Bible in lieu of reading the Word.

The upward look of supplication. We also learn from Jude 20 that we are to be "praying in the Holy Spirit." What does it mean to "pray in the Holy Spirit?" Jack Taylor, in his book *Prayer: Life's Limitless Reach*, writes about the "cycle of prayer." That is, true prayer does not begin with us, but at the throne of God. The Bible says, "We do not know what we should pray for as we ought" (Romans 8:26). Therefore, God takes the initiative and impresses upon our hearts, by His Spirit, and often through His Word, the things for which we should pray. The apostle continues by saying, "Likewise, the Spirit also helps in our weaknesses. . . . The Spirit Himself makes intercession for us with groanings which cannot be uttered. Now he who searches the hearts knows what the mind of the Spirit is, because he makes intercession for the saints according to the will of God" (Romans 8:26-27).

No matter how grounded you or I might be in the Word of God, if we seek to overcome apostasy in our own strength, we will be defeated. We need the upward look of supplication. It is sad that not many of us today know much about this matter of "praying in the Holy Spirit." Quite honestly, I must admit that experientially I am far more knowledgeable about building up myself in the Word of God than I am in praying in the Holy Spirit.

I am convinced that one of modern day Christianity's biggest blessings is, in many ways, one of its greatest curses in disguise. We are inundated with printed materials and cassette tapes about our Christian faith. We can walk into any Christian bookstore and find dozens, if not scores, of books written about prayer. It's interesting that when we read the book of Acts, we read about the greatest prayer warriors of all time. Those early believers called down heaven and opened prison doors with prayer. They knew the shortest way to anyone's heart was through the throne of grace. Yet, they never read books on how to pray. They didn't attend prayer seminars or have a tape series on prayer. They simply prayed. And when they prayed, they prayed in the Spirit. Today we know it all in theory, but not enough of us know it in experience.

Many of us would do well to ask our Lord the same

question the disciples asked him so long ago on a Galilean hillside, "Lord, teach us to pray" (Luke 11:1). The disciples knew if they could ever learn to pray as Jesus prayed, then preaching with power and other needs of the ministry would simply be by-products.

We need the Spirit's help to pray according to the will of God. John revealed that "this is the confidence that we have in Him, that if we ask anything according to His will, He hears us. And if we know that He hears us, whatever we ask, we know we have the petitions that we have asked of Him" (1 John 5:14-15).[4] James said it this way, "You ask and do not receive, because you ask amiss, that you may spend it on you pleasures" (4:3). Our Lord Himself prayed in Gethesemane's garden saying "not My will, but Yours be done" (Luke 22:42).

In contrast to praying in the Spirit, some pray in the flesh, according to their own worldly desires. It is no wonder their prayers are not answered. Others pray in the soulish realm. They are worked up emotionally but it's all over after "the experience" has passed away. The prayer that keeps us in the love of God is prayer in the Spirit.

We will go down in defeat if we are not insulated in the love of God through the Word of God and through prayer. Both are vitally important, and are meant to go together. The Bible without prayer has no dynamic. Prayer without the Bible has no direction.

The forward look of anticipation. True believers are "looking for the mercy of our Lord Jesus Christ unto eternal life" (Jude 21). To be insulated by the love of God in these days of apostasy, it is not enough to merely look back; we must also look forward. As believers, we have something to look forward to. Jude alludes to the Second Coming of Christ here because apostasy is one of the major signs of the last days which signal the Lord's return from glory.

Eager anticipation of the return of our blessed Lord will keep us insulated in the love of God in the days of apostasy.

In his letter to Titus, Paul referred to this great event: "Looking for the blessed hope and glorious appearing of our great God and Savior Jesus Christ" (2:13). But today, few who profess Jesus Christ seem to be looking for Him. In fact, some give the impression that the mention of the Second Coming is a bit old-fashioned.

Jude reveals that this is one of the reasons some are not keeping themselves in the love of God. They have no forward look of anticipation. As believers look for our Savior, the Lord Jesus Christ, it makes a difference in the way they live. When they are sincerely looking for Christ to return at any time, it moves them to live a godly life.

There are a lot of believers that never get past the cross in their Christian experience. It is important to look back in appreciation, but it is also important to look forward in anticipation. The way to keep insulated is to keep our eyes on Jesus who said, "If I go . . . I will come again and receive you to myself (John 14:3)."

These three words—building, praying, looking—are present-tense participles. That simply means they should continually characterize our behavior.

BE SEPARATED

It is not enough to be educated or insulated; we must also be separated. We are not speaking here of a hard, cold separation, but of a warm living sacrifice consumed with love for the lost. Paul put it this way, "I beseech you, therefore, brethren, by the mercies of God, that you present your bodies a living sacrifice, holy, acceptable to God, which is your reasonable service. And do not be conformed to this world, but be transformed by the renewing of your mind, that you may prove what is that good and acceptable and perfect will of God" (Romans 12:1-2). To that we can add Jude's words, "And on some have compassion, making a distinction; but others save with fear, pulling them out of the fire, hating even the garment defiled by the flesh" (Jude 22-23).

The church today is too often silent with its witness. What should be our response to those who are influenced by the spirit of apostasy? We should respond to them sympathetically, for one of the most hypocritical things in the world is orthodoxy without compassion. A lot of people who speak the truth today do not do it in love. Our admonition from Paul through the Ephesian epistle is to "speak the truth in love." Thus, Jude turns now to reveal to us that we are to be soul winners. We are to have compassion. And, the best way to do this is to be living a separated life that is a warm living sacrifice. We must be educated, insulated, and separated.

Many Christians today have lost their concern, their compassion for souls. The reason is that they are living separated lives. Many have lost their tears. Once a young captain in the Salvation Army wrote to General Booth, their godly and soul-winning founder, saying, "I'm not seeing any converts. People do not seem to be responding to my message." General Booth replied by telegram with only two words—"Try tears." There is a dire need for the Christian in these days of apostasy to deal with the lost in a sympathetic sense.

There are three groups of people who need our witness. Jude refers to them as sincere doubters, those living on the very edge of hell, and those who are deeply contaminated by sin. In other words, there are some who need to be dealt with compassionately; others, courageously; and still others, cautiously.

We need to deal with apostates compassionately. Jude says, "On some have compassion, making a distinction." The phrase "making a distinction" is properly translated in some versions as "sincere doubters." We should approach sincere doubters in a compassionate way. A lot of people today are like Simon Peter, walking on the water. He started out doing well until fear gripped his heart. As doubt began to set in, he began to sink. He cried out, "Lord, save me." Jesus reached out his hand, and at once they were back in the security of the boat. Jesus' question was, "O, ye of little faith, why did you doubt?" There are many today like Peter, slowly sinking. Oh, that more of God's people would reach out to them and "have compassion." Orthodoxy is useless without compassion. Someone has said, "People do not care how much we know until they know how much we care." The word *compassion* comes from two Latin words: *com*, which means "with"; and *passion*, which means "to suffer." Therefore, compassion literally means to put one's self in the place of another; to suffer with that person. It is one of the lost words of our Christian vocabulary.

Many Christians see others today in the same manner as the man that Jesus touched in Mark 8. This blind man could see with the first touch, but said, "I see men but they look like trees walking." So blurred was his vision that he could not tell a man from a tree. He was too blind to discern the condition of those he saw. As a result he was unable to help others.

We are no different than that blind man. All too often we are interested only in our own jobs, churches, families, theology, orthodoxy, and pain. It's me, me, me; mine, mine, mine; and ours, ours, ours! We see *me* without really seeing them. But when Jesus touched the blind man a second time, he said, "I see every man clearly." That is where the church ought to be in these days of apostasy. We need the touch of Jesus that helps us to reach out in compassion.

We need to deal with apostates courageously. According to Jude, "Others save with fear, pulling them out of the fire" (v. 23). This group is further gone than the sincere doubters, for those who need to be "pulled out of the fire" are obviously closer to the flames of hell. To witness about Christ to this kind of individual requires a much stronger and bolder stand. They should be approached courageously by the believer. No case should be regarded as hopeless, for no one is beyond the reach of God. However, to reclaim those so near the fire, a real sense of urgency is needed. Just as a man plucks a brand out of the fire, this type of individual is to be confronted in boldness and courage.

The fire about which Jude speaks is eternal fire. It is amazing how silent pulpits are regarding the biblical doctrine of hell. The Bible speaks clearly about the reality of hell and offers vivid descriptions of it. "And do not fear those who kill the body but cannot kill the soul. But rather fear Him who is able to destroy both soul and body in hell" (Matthew 10:28). "The Son of Man will send out his angels, and they will gather out of His kingdom all things that offend, and those who practice lawlessness, and will cast them into the furnace of fire. There will be wailing and gnashing of teeth" (13:41-42). "Then He will also say to those on the left hand, 'Depart from Me, you cursed, into the everlasting fire prepared for the devil and his angels'" (25:41). "And these will go away into everlasting punishment, but the righteous into eternal life" (25:46). Who was this preacher? The Lord Jesus Himself! In fact, He spent far more time warning about the dangers of hell than He did speaking of the glories of heaven.

These days some Christians are not sure what they believe about hell. General William Booth once said that he wished he could send all of his candidates for officership to hell for twenty-four hours as part of their training. He was convinced that only in this way could they develop the needed compassion to win the lost to a saving faith in Jesus Christ and save them "with fear, pulling them out of the fire." Surely this is what Fanny Crosby had in mind when she penned these penetrating words:

> Rescue the perishing, care for the dying,
> Snatch them in pity from sin and the grave;

Weep o'er the erring one, lift up the fallen,
Tell them of Jesus, the mighty to save.

Down in the human heart, crushed by the tempter,
Feelings lie buried that grace can restore;
Touched by a loving heart, wakened by kindness
Chords that are broken will vibrate once more.

Rescue the perishing, care for the dying;
Jesus is merciful, Jesus will save.

We need to deal with apostates cautiously. Jude says that
we are to hate "even the garment defiled by the flesh" (v.
22). Those who have departed the faith are to be approached with fear. Some sins and some sinners may not
merely threaten the spiritual life of the soul winner, but
actually snare the servant of Christ. That is why it is so vital
to be separated. More than one well meaning man or woman with a heart for God has fallen into the trap of Satan in
trying to witness to those whose garments were "defiled by
the flesh." We must avoid allowing our compassion and
courage to overshadow our caution!

As we deal with apostates we must take care to never
get caught in the compromise trap. We should never compromise to win someone to the Lord Jesus Christ. Occasion-
ally we hear of a Christian seeking to justify a certain sin to
"win over the sinner." We don't find that in the Bible! Some
believe that the way to win the social elite is to compromise
with their life-style. Many a Christian has fallen prey to
that philosophy. Some have lost their effectiveness in evan-
gelism through covetousness. But the Bible says, "Do not
overwork to be rich; because of your own understanding,
cease!" (Proverbs 23:4). Others are tempted to "water down"
the gospel so as not to offend those with whom they are
trying to witness. We need to take great pains not to compromise the gospel of our Lord Jesus Christ.

We see great concern today regarding AIDS. It has
gripped our society with fear. People are fearful of blood

transfusions and even casual contact. Would to God His own people feared sin in the same way as they go about their work and witness. That is what Jude is calling us to do when he says, "On some, have compassion, making a distinction; but others, save with fear, pulling them out of the fire, hating even the garment defiled by the flesh" (Jude 22-23).

Solomon said, "He that winneth souls is wise." I'm so thankful that Johnny Keeton took the time as a seventeen-year-old young man to approach me after a basketball game to tell me about Jesus. He did it compassionately and courageously and, I might add, cautiously. He led me to a saving knowledge of Jesus Christ.

Somewhere are people to be reached for Christ that no one else can reach quite as you can. Perhaps, some are sincere doubters who should be approached with compassion. Perhaps some are living in open rebellion in sin, on the very edge of hell and should be dealt with with courage and urgency. Or perhaps, they are wallowing in the filth of sin and should be approached with caution. May God grant that, as authentic believers, we be educated, insulated, and separated so we might deal with the lost in a sympathetic sense. Orthodoxy without compassion is sheer hypocrisy.

The story is told of a lady who left her small boy asleep in the backseat of her car while she made a quick stop at a local store. Upon returning, she found the car gone. Within an hour dozens of people were involved in the search for her boy. A short time later the car was found, but without the boy. As darkness approached and panic began to set in, one of the search volunteers, a veteran of the Vietnam War, thought to himself, *Perhaps, this was not a kidnapping at all, but someone who simply stole an automobile, unaware of the child until he had driven away.* The Vietnam vet took a flashlight and walked up a dirt road not far from where the car had been found. He spotted an abandoned house with its windows boarded up. The swing on the porch was stacked with what looked to be newspapers and a silhouette of someone lying in the swing. He shined the flashlight toward the swing and called out, "Billy!"

Quick came the reply, "Is that you, Daddy?"

The vet replied, "No, Billy, I am not your daddy, but I'm here to take you to your daddy!" That, friend, illustrates the job of the church. We are to rescue the perishing. It was for that cause that our Lord Jesus Christ came into this world, and it is for that cause that the church exists.

As we safeguard against imposters in the church we must purpose to be educated, insulated, and separated. But let us not forget that we need to be consistent with our calling; and that is to win the lost.

ENDNOTES:

1. Maxwell Coder, *Jude, The Acts of the Apostates* (Chicago: Moody, 1958), p. 106.

2. John MacArthur, Jr., *Beware the Pretenders*. (Wheaton, Ill.: Victor, 1980), p. 90.

3. Alexander Maclaren, *Expositions of Holy Scripture*, 17 vols. (Grand Rapids: Baker, 1982), 17:97.

4. Warren Wiersbe, *Be Alert* (Wheaton, Ill.: Victor Books, 1984), p. 160.

EIGHT
THE BASIS FOR OUR HOPE

We have said much about apostasy, the work of impostors in the church. We have studied this "falling away" from many angles. And in all of this we have focused on the false believer as the one falling. That is because the Bible clearly teaches that it is not the genuine believer who falls from grace. In fact, the very phrase "falling from grace" is a misnomer. Grace is God's unmerited favor and we do not fall from it. We fall into grace!

As we have examined the issue of apostasy we have drawn much from the words of Jude. It is significant that he begins and ends his epistle with some of the strongest words in the Bible about the security of the believer in Christ. During most of his letter Jude addresses his readers in the third person. As he closes he moves to the second person as if to get more personal in closing.[1] He ends his letter with a note of hope for these dark days of apostasy by saying, "Now to Him who is able to keep you from stumbling, and to present you faultless before the presence of His glory with exceeding joy, to God our Savior, who alone is wise, be glory and majesty, dominion and power, both now and forever. Amen" (Jude 24-25). Jude is telling us that we have hope in overcoming apostasy.

Our hope is rooted in two very important truths. First,

it is rooted in the sovereignty of God. Sometimes it appears that the spirit of apostasy is winning out. But no! God is able. He is omniscient, omnipresent, and omnipotent. Second, our hope is rooted in the security of the believer. As we see the effects of apostasy today we might be tempted to worry about our own salvation. But no! We are secure in Christ in the now life and in the next life.

THE SOVEREIGNTY OF GOD

We are not talking about a God whose heroics are confined to bygone days. Nor are we talking about a God who is powerless. Jude does not say, He *was* able or *shall* be able; but rather that He *is* able. Right now! He was able in the past and He will be able in the future, but the good news is that He is able in the now.

We do not use the word *sovereignty* much today. Those influenced by a spirit of apostasy stand at arms length from it because they do not want a God who rules over them. The Bible speaks of a king who is able to do what He wants to do. Perhaps sovereignty is best defined by saying that God does what He pleases and is always pleased with what He does.

What is your need? Is it grace? "And God is able to make all grace abound toward you, that you, always having all sufficiency in all things, may have an abundance for every good work" (2 Corinthians 9:8). Is it the need to overcome temptation? "For in that He Himself has suffered, being tempted, He is able to aid those who are tempted" (Hebrews 2:18). Is it the need for salvation? "Therefore He is also able to save to the uttermost those who come to God through Him, since He always lives to make intercession for them" (Hebrews 7:25). Is it the need of security? "For this reason I also suffer these things; nevertheless I am not ashamed, for I know whom I have believed and am persuaded that He is able to keep what I have committed to

Him until that Day" (2 Timothy 1:12). Some of us are like the man to whom Jesus prefaced His healing by saying, "Do you believe that I am able to do this?" (Matthew 9:28). He is able!

Are we ever left without this hope? No. It stands to reason that if God can keep us for one minute, He can keep us forever. Note the words of Jude, "both now and forever" (v. 24). That truth spans all points of time. No matter what transpires, God is soverign.

The church today is in danger of infiltration and undermining by those who are influenced by the spirit of apostasy. We must constantly take heed of Jude's warning us against this danger. He clearly reminds us that the only source of power for combating apostasy is in the sovereignty of God.

The Word of God can be our strength as we combat the spirit of apostasy. We need to draw often from the truths of the benediction in Jude 24-25, which aptly describe God's greatness.

Our limited human language cannot begin to fully describe the meaning of the four words Jude uses in verse 25 in this final crescendo—"glory and majesty, dominion, and power." Who can adequately describe the glory of God? Who can even begin to describe the majesty of God? These words remind us that God is sovereign and emphasize that truth by focusing on His omniscience, omnipresence, and omnipotence.

Our God is omniscient. He is wise and knows all. Our God is omnipresent. He is everywhere present—"both now and forever." The psalmist said it best: "Such knowledge is to wonderful for me; it is high, I cannot attain it. Where can I go from Your spirit? Or where can I flee from Your presence? If I ascend into heaven, You are there; if I make my bed in hell, behold You are there. If I take the wings of the morning, and dwell in the uttermost parts of the sea, even there Your hand shall lead me, and Your right hand shall hold me" (Psalm 139:6-10). Our God is omnipotent. He has all power and all authority.

The words of Jude 24-25 are an impressive reminder of the greatness of our God. I believe Jude knew that if we could grasp these truths we would never be deceived or led astray by apostates or other false teachers.

THE SECURITY OF THE BELIEVER

Given the state of the church today, it is understandable that some believers might fear for their personal security. Perhaps that is why Jude began and ended his letter with the message of the security of the believer. Jude provides the believer hope by teaching two facts about the security of the believer. He reminds us that we are secure in the now and in the next life.

We are secure in the now life. In Jude's words, "Now to Him who is able to keep you from stumbling" (v. 24). It is wonderful to know that one day He will "present us faultless before the throne." But how encouraging to know that in the meantime, He is able to keep us from stumbling.

We live in an uncertain world. It is unstable politically, economically, materially, socially, nationally, and internationally. But amid all this uncertainty God promises to "keep you from stumbling." Our family's moving to Fort Lauderdale was an unforgettable experience. Those early weeks were often difficult. The hustle and bustle of a metropolitan area of more than a million people was a far cry from the quiet little Oklahoma town we had called home only a few weeks earlier. Our oldest daughter, Wendy, was four years old at the time. I remember vividly how each time we would leave our home and drive in the strange surroundings with its endless lines of traffic, how obsessed she was with the question with which I would be continually bombarded, "We will be able to get home, won't we, Daddy?" That is very important for a child. That is, to know he will be able to get home. It is also very important for a child of God.

How important to know we are going to be able to get home. How important it is to know that we do not have to wonder from day to day if we are saved or lost. How important it is to know that God will keep us from stumbling. Yes, indeed, we are secure in the now life.

We are secure in the next life. In Jude's words, God will "present you faultless before the presence of His glory with exceeding joy" (Jude 24). No one is faultless today. We all have our spots and wrinkles. But one day true believers are going to be like the Lord Jesus. And in that day (because of His blood) we will stand before the throne "faultless." The Bible says, "Beloved, now we are children of God; and it has not yet been revealed what we shall be, but we know that when He is revealed, we shall be like Him, for we shall see Him as He is" (1 John 3:2).

When we receive Jesus Christ into our lives, we are immediately justified in spirit. But as we grow in Christ's grace and knowledge, we become progressively sanctified in the soul. One day we will be presented faultless before the throne—justified, sanctified, and glorified! The apostle Paul deals with this subject in Ephesians when he says, "That He might sanctify and cleanse her with the washing of water by the word, that He might present her to himself a glorious church, not having spot or wrinkle or any such thing, but that she should be holy and without blemish" (5:26-27).

It is important to note that both Paul and Jude use the same Greek word *amonos,* which means "without blemish," to describe our condition when we are presented to the bridegroom. The same word is used by the Lord Jesus Himself in Peter's epistle when He says, "Knowing that you were not redeemed with corruptible things, like silver or gold, from your aimless conduct received by tradition from your fathers, but with the precious blood of Christ, as of a lamb without blemish and without spot" (1 Peter 1:18-19).

This is what John meant when He said, "Beloved, now we are children of God, and it has not yet been revealed what we shall be, but we know that when He is revealed, we shall be like Him for we shall see Him as He is" (1 John 3:2).[2]

John got a glimpse of this one day from his lonely island called Patmos and said, "And I heard, as it were, the voice of a great multitude, as the sound of many waters and as the sound of mighty thunderings, saying, 'Alleluia! For the Lord God omnipotent reigns! Let us be glad and rejoice and give Him glory, for the marriage of the Lamb has come, and His wife has made herself ready.' " (Revelation 19:6-7).

That great day is going to be the marriage supper of the Lamb. Our understanding of Jewish weddings in biblical times throws considerable light on this feast. The first stage of the wedding was the marriage covenant. The groom would leave his father's house and travel to his prospective bride to settle and pay a ransom price. Once the agreement was made, that signaled the second stage and the bride and groom would drink wine as a symbol of unity. Now, they were considered married although they did not begin to live together. The groom had to prepare a place for his bride. The third stage began when the groom, who had prepared the place, returned at an unannounced time. When people in the neighborhood saw him coming they would shout, "Behold, the bridegroom cometh!" Thus they would forewarn the bride to get ready. The final stage entailed the groom getting the bride and taking her to his father's house for the wedding ceremony. There he would present her before the father.

What an obvious picture of that day when our Lord Jesus will "present us faultless" before the throne. Just as the Jewish bridegroom left his father's house, traveled to the home of the prospective bride to pay the ransom price, so the Lord Jesus Christ, two thousand years ago, left the glories of heaven and His Father's house to enter this sin-cursed earth to pay the price of our salvation. He purchased us with His own blood on Calvary—"For you were bought with a price; therefore glorify God in your body and in your spirit, which are God's" (1 Corinthians 6:20). On the evening before His crucifixion, Jesus took the cup as a symbol of our unity with Him. Just as the Jewish bridegroom returned to his father's house to prepare a place for his bride, so the Lord Jesus Christ, before Calvary, declared, "I go to prepare a place for you, and if I go and prepare a place for you, I will come again and receive you to Myself; that where I am there you may be also" (John 14:2-3).

Just as the Jewish bridegroom returned at an unannounced time to receive his bride, so the Lord Jesus Christ at an unannounced time and with a loud shout will receive his bride. And, just as people would begin to shout, "Behold, the bridegroom cometh," many in pulpits across the world are making that shout heard loud and clear today. As Bible prophecies are fulfilled and events point to the coming of Christ, many faithful preachers are beginning to shout, "Behold, the bridegroom cometh." And finally, just as the Jewish bridegroom received his new bride and took her away to the father's house for the wedding, so the Lord Jesus Christ will come and receive us, and take us away to the great marriage supper of the Lamb. At that time He will "present us faultless before the presence of His glory with exceeding joy."

What should be our response as believers? When a bride is about to be married, as we are to Christ, she takes two important courses of action. First, she accepts the invitation of the bridegroom. Obviously, without this acceptance there would be no wedding. Second, she makes herself as lovely as she can for the ceremony. My questions to you are, have you accepted the invitation of your bridegroom, the Lord Jesus Christ? If so, are you making yourself as lovely as you can for the wedding? Are you keeping yourself in the love of Christ?

Jesus will receive His bride with exceeding joy. One day the Lord Jesus will have the special joy of presenting His bride before the Father's throne. Incidentally, it was the anticipation of this joy that helped Him endure the agony of the cross experience. This is what the Bible means when it says, "Looking unto Jesus, the author and finisher of our faith, who for the joy that was set before Him endured the cross, despising the shame, and has sat down at the right hand of the throne of God" (Hebrews 12:2). This was the "joy" that was set before him.[3] That is, to present you faultless before the presence of his glory with exceeding joy. What a faithful and loving bridegroom is our Lord Jesus Christ.

It is one thing for Jesus to keep us from falling, but quite another to present us "faultless" before the throne. We can never make ourselves faultless, but the Lord Jesus can. He has opened a fountain for sin where we can wash and be clean.

> There is a fountain filled with blood
> Drawn from Emmanuel's veins;
> And sinners, plunged beneath that flood,
> Lose all their guilty stains.
>
> Dear dying Lamb, thy precious blood shall
>   never lose its power,
> 'Til all the ransomed church of God
> Be saved, to sin no more,
>
> And since, by faith I saw the stream
> Thy flowing wounds supply,
> Redeeming love has been my theme
> And shall be 'til I die.
>
> William Cowper

After all is said and done, God is sovereign and we are secure—"both now and forever." However, in a very real sense all has not been said and done. We, the church of Jesus Christ, have a part. We must never cease to earnestly contend for the faith which was once for all delivered to the saints. And how? By loving the faith. By learning the faith. By living the faith. And by loosing the faith. That charge was delivered to the church, and no one else will be responsible . . . if the foundations be destroyed!

As we remain faithful in our work and witness, those imposters among us will be . . . unmasked!

ENDNOTES:

1. Lange, *Lange's Commentary on The Holy Scriptures,* 12 vols. (Grand Rapids: Zondervan, 1960), 12:33.

2. Maxwell Coder, *Jude the Acts of the Apostates* (Chicago: Moody, 1958), p. 124.

3. James Smith and Robert Lee, *Handfuls on Purpose,* 12 vols. (Grand Rapids: Eerdmans, 1947), 12:156.